INDIA
Communication Policy
and
Strategy for Development

About the Editors

Padma Rani (Ph.D. Sociology, 1997, Jawaharlal Nehru University, New Delhi) is a communication researcher and teacher at School of Communication, MAHE, Manipal. She is the coordinator of Media Research Centre. She has conducted funded research projects from NCW& UNFPA. Her areas of interest are Information communication technology with special interest in the area of Digital media. She is guiding Ph.D. research in the area. She has presented research papers in various international conferences like IAMCR and AMIC. She was awarded a DAAD scholarship for teaching media and communication studies at Bremen, Germany. She was invited in 2016 as a visiting professor to the Technical University of Nuremberg. She teaches both under-graduate and post-graduate students of communication and media studies.

Binod C. Agrawal (Ph.D. Anthropology, 1970, University of Wisconsin, Madison, USA) is a well-known International Communication Research expert. He has a reputation of being innovative in research methods and techniques, institution building, management and teaching leadership. Founder Director of several institutions and a university. Earlier he worked for over two decades and pioneered use of qualitative methods for communication research during the world famous Satellite Instructional Television Experiment (SITE), 1975-76 and led an interdisciplinary SITE social research team of over 100 social scientists. Author of two dozen books and several dozen articles in national and International Journals and continues to publish. He is currently the Mentor of Media Research Centre at School of Communication, Manipal Academy of Higher Education, Manipal.

INDIA
Communication Policy and Strategy for Development

Edited by:
Padma Rani
Binod C. Agrawal

CONCEPT PUBLISHING COMPANY PVT. LTD.
NEW DELHI-110059

ISBN-13: 978-93-88937-90-0

First Published 2021

Published and Printed by

Concept Since 1974

Concept Publishing Company Pvt. Ltd.
A/15-16, Commercial Block, Mohan Garden,
New Delhi-110059 (INDIA)
T : 91 11 25351460, 91 11 25351794
E : publishing@conceptpub.com; *W* : www.conceptpub.com

Cataloging in Publication Data--Courtesy: D.K. Agencies (P) Ltd. <docinfo@dkagencies.com>

India: Communication Policy and Strategy for Development (Conference) (2017 : Manipala, India)

India : communication policy and strategy for development / edited by Padma Rani, Binod C. Agrawal.

pages cm

Papers presented at the international conference on the theme, 'India: Communication Policy and Strategy for Development', organized by Media Research Centre, School of Communication, Manipal Academy of Higher Education, held during March 17-18, 2017.

Includes bibliographical references and index.

ISBN 9789388937900

1. Communication policy—India—Congresses. 2. Communication in economic development—India—Congresses. 3. Communication—Social aspects—India—Congresses. I. Padma Rani, editor. II. Agrawal, Binod C., 1942- editor. III. Manipal Academy of Higher Education. Media Research Centre, organizer. IV. Title.

LCC P92.I4I53 2017 | DDC 302.230954 23

Preface

Manipal Institute of Communication (earlier known as School of Communication) has been consistently ranked within the ten best colleges in India under the colleges offering Mass communication and journalism courses. The school has a number of international collaborations to boast off in the areas of student exchange and faculty exchange. In March 2016 in the inaugural of the National Seminar, the Vice-Chancellor announced the setting up of the Media Research Centre. It was first of its kind under the university set up in India. The Media Research Centre was formally inaugurated in October, 2016. The vision of the centre is to be to establish a centre of excellence for research in communication and media.

The Media Research Centre is greatly indebted to the Vice-Chancellor of Manipal Academy of Higher Education Dr. H. Vinod Bhat for his vision to establish a centre exclusively for media and communication studies. The centre was given an intra-mural grant of 15 lakh Indian rupees out of which we were able to conduct the seminar.

To celebrate the first anniversary of its inception, the Media Research Centre organised the International conference. The theme of the conference was India: Communication Policy and Strategy for Development. The conference had members participating from SAARC countries and Malaysia. The conference provided us an opportunity to discuss the needs for a communication policy and strategy. The conference was inaugurated by the Registrar of MAHE Dr. Narayana Sabhahit.

The keynote for the conference was delivered by Rohan Samarajiva founding Chair of LIRNEasia, an Asian infrastructure policy and regulation think tank, and Chair of Communication Policy Research south which seeks to develop policy intellectuals in Africa and Asia. He has been deeply engaged in the challenges of taking research to policy through the former organization and in the formation of scholars who understand policy processes and are motivated to contribute to them through the latter.

Nirmalmani Adhikary gave us an idea about communication models from ancient texts. Md. Golam Rahman and Mariam Sheikh provided us with inputs from Bangladesh and Pakistan. The Technical sessions provided us the opportunity to discuss on the needs and quality of communication in order to prosper, because a country needs a great communication system. Investment in communication yields a tremendous return, well informed citizens make better and, well-informed choices.

The invited speakers—Buroshiva Dasgupta, Bashabi Fraser, Md. Golam Rahman, Nirmalmani Adhikary, Ashoka Dias, Chandrabhanu Patnayak, Mariam Sheikh and Wan Aida Wan Yahya there talks have been transcribed and printed in the book. The paper presenters who gave us their complete paper on the scheduled time have been included in the publication.

Acknowledgements

The book involves selected papers presented at the international conference held in Manipal on 'India: Communication Policy and Strategy for Development' from March 17 to March 18, 2017 in which especially South Asian scholars were invited. First and foremost, we like sincerely to thank Manipal Academy of Higher Education (MAHE), Vice Chancellor Dr. H. Vinod Bhat for his support and guidance to the Media Research Centre at the School of Communication, Manipal.

The key note address was given by Prof. Rohan Samarajiva followed by various other presentations by the scholars from across India, Bangladesh, Nepal, Sri Lanka, Pakistan and Malaysia. We are grateful to the authors who accepted our invitation and came to Manipal to present their papers.

The organizing responsibility was with Media Research Centre, School of Communication (SOC), Manipal Academy of Higher Education (MAHE). We are grateful to Dr. H.S. Shubha and Dr. Manjushree for their immense help in organizing the conference. The logistic and academic support was largely taken care by the editors of the book, Dr. Padma Rani and Dr. Binod C. Agrawal supported by the SOC staff. Mr. Balaji, A.C., Mr. Praseed Nair, Mr. Padmakumar, K. and the Research scholars Mr. Vijay Kumar and Mr. Deepak, B.J.; we are grateful to them for their immense help.

The logistic arrangements for the stay of the participants was offered at the international guest house of MAHE, the staff were very kind to take care the guests coming both from India and abroad. We acknowledge their valuable help in taking care of the guests.

Last but not the least, help was provided by MAHE administration to ensure the success of the conference. We are grateful to them.

We are greatly indebted to Dr. Manjushree for following up with various paper presenters and putting the manuscript together and the repeated reminders about the deadline to us.

Contents

List of Contributors

Ashoka Dias (Dr.), Director, MTV and MBC, MN Channel (P) Limited. Ashok Dias is the country representative of Asian Media and Communication Research Centre (AMIC).

Binod C., Agrawal (M.S. 1969, Ph.D. 1970, University of Wisconsin, Madison, USA), M.A., Anthropology 1963, Lucknow University, India) is a well-known International Communication Research Expert.

Buroshiva Dasgupta (Dr.), Former Professor/Director, NSHM, Institute of Media and Design (NIMD), Kolkata, Formerly, Professor/Director, Manipal Institute of Communication, Karnataka, India, Formerly Resident Editor, Financial Express, Kolkata. Buroshiva Dasgupta has been a practising journalist for over 25 years in the media in various capacities.

Chandrabhanu Patnayak (Dr.) is the Organizing Secretary, Peoples Education Council and Peoples Education Conference (held in September 2018, Bhubaneswar) and is the Director, Institute of Knowledge Societies, Centurion University, Bhubaneshwar.

Geetha A.J. is a Lecturer in Department of Mass Communication & Journalism in Alva's College in Moodubidire, Karnataka.

Golam Rahman (Dr.), Ph.D. was a Professor in the Department of Mass Communication and Journalism (MO) at the University of Dhaka, Bangladesh. Currently, Dr. Rahman is serving as the Chief Information Commissioner (CIC) of Information Commission, Bangladesh.

Mariam Sheikh (Dr.) is a Ph.D. in Communication from Florida State University and a Fulbright Scholar. By profession she is a career civil servant working for the Federal Government of Pakistan.

Moulya Jeevanram (Dr.) is an Associate Professor in Department of PG Studies in Journalism in Alva's College in Moodubidire, Karnataka.

Nirmala Mani Adhikary (Dr.) is a prominent communication theorist from Nepal, who is acclaimed for the Sadharanikaran Model of Communication and the theory of Sancharyoga. Dr. Adhikary is one of the most cited communication theorists in the very recent years.

P.V. Sangeetha (Dr.) is an Assistant Professor in Department of Visual Communication, Shri S.S. Shasun Jain college for Women, Chennai.

Rohan Samarajiva (Prof.) is founding Chair of LIRNEasia, an Asian infrastructure policy and regulation think tank, and Chair of Community Policy Research South which seeks to develop policy intellectuals in Africa and Asia.

Sathwik is a Student of Master of Arts in Journalism & Mass Communication in Alva's College in Moodubidire, Karnataka.

Shrigouri S. Jhosi is a Student in Department of PG Studies in Journalism and Mass Communication, Alva's College, Moodubidire, Karnataka.

Srinivasa Pejathaya is an Assitant Professor in Department of Mass Communication & Journalism in Alva's College, Moodubidire, Karnataka.

Sushmitha is a final year student of Post-graduation in Department of Mass Communication & Journalism in Alva's College, Moodubidire, Karnataka.

T.R. Ramakrishnan (Dr.), Ph.D. is a faculty at the Jain Group of Institutions (Jain University), Bengaluru.

V. Anashwara is a Visual Analyst in Mckinsey & Company, Chennai.

Vishakha Mandrawadkar is Student of Mass Communication & Journalism in Alva's College in Moodubidire, Karnataka.

Wan Aida Wan Yahya (Prof.) is a Senior Lecturer attached with the Faculty of Film, Theatre and Animation, Universiti Teknologi MARA, Malaysia. Currently she holds the post of Head of Academic Accreditation at the Office of Academic Affairs.

Introduction

The making of policies in response to the development in the communication infrastructure has happened across the globe. Some policies were made in response to specific events, while others were well-thought-out. Policies developed at different levels-local, regional and international; have affected the relationship between people and nations.

The communication policy in some countries is piecemeal. They set norms and guidelines for a particular medium or a specific sector. These norms or guidelines are partial and conflicting. The different sectors need to bring together and a positive integration between different sectors. There should be an integrated communication policy rather than having a piecemeal approach. The integrated policy is required as parts overlap with each other within a particular sector and also with other sectors. Therefore, it is necessary to have a cumulative communication policy.

Drawing on the experiences from other countries makes it easier to recognize the potential for policy fcrmulation and planning and its implications. In the formulation of communication policy, it is necessary that a country recognizes its existence as part of the global communication system. The basis for national policy should be a fair and equitable distribution of the world's wealth of information, knowledge and culture. The policy should also address the existing imbalances, especially to improve the quality of life of its people. Countries can design policy not only for themselves but also for sub-regional or regional groups for the sake of cooperation.

As a general rule, policy formulation entails determination of the main goals and roles of communication media and other associated communication systems. Policy formulation may require reorganization of systems. The steps involved in the implementation of policy are evaluation, assessment, reassessment and refinement. The policy steps should fit into overall national policy and goals.

The need for a communication policy is due to the tremendous strides made in communication technology and the impact of such technological developments on the entire fabric of a given society both internally and its relationship with other societies. The growing sophistication of communication technology has led to changes in communication activities and information flow. The philosophy and communication models adopted by societies existed outside their systems. Over some time, the gaps in these adapted systems have become evident as societies have their own needs as per their social, economic and cultural patterns. Therefore, the communication policy-makers have to take into account the economic problems, social problems, the national goals and programmes while framing a holistic policy.

India should aim at setting up a national communication policy council which could act as a coordinating body between different sectors of communication and media. The council should formulate a policy, implement and carry out arbitration if required and supported by an adequate executive, technical services. National Council should act as the nodal body for the implementation of the communication policy and lay down the strategy. Such a national council could assign research tasks, collate information and stimulate exploratory discussions at many levels. Subsequently, it could elaborate policies or advise thereon for government and communication institutions. It can be fully operational only if it is permanent and provided with requisite finance and personnel.

The principal functions of a national communication policy council would include:

(i) to promote coherent, national and comprehensive analyses of existing policies and controls and national communication objectives; to identify the rights, interests, obligations and interdependence of various communication institutions within society;

(ii) to enhance greater efficiency in the application and expenditures of frequently limited economic and physical resources by setting priorities and reducing internal contradictions;

(iii) to safeguard the rights of various sectors involved in communication enterprises by providing a forum for continuous discussion and clarification;

(iv) to provide the framework for anticipating changes in media technology, assessing their value for promoting national and international goals, and revealing their harmful effects; to perform a "lookout" function to foresee technological innovations on the international scene which may be necessary, as "quantum jumps" in national communication planning;

(v) to identify crucial international communication policy issues which are constraints on national policy;

(vi) to ensure national compatibility with international norms and standards:

(vii) to enable the nation to speak consistently and coherently at international discussions of communication matters, and to recommend appropriate diplomatic action on questions involving international communication.

The implementation of communication policies requires joint action from other sectors of a country. The national communication policy is not to control the media. It can be successful if there is a system for a constant dialogue with citizens, whose participation is essential for the success of communication policy.

History of Communication Policy in India

In 1947, the Indian government adopted a developmental model of governance intending to improve the health, economic and educational conditions of the people. The National Planning Committee had development communication as a priority. Therefore, the planners explored the idea of the use of radio for information and awareness all across the country.

In the post-Nehruvian era, Vikram Sarabhai was of the view that

India should have the know-how of all the technologies for all-round growth and development. The SITE programme was launched with the support of the then Prime Minister Indira Gandhi so that television could reach rural areas. The programme design kept the socio-cultural background of the areas in mind. Radio and television were sources of entertainment, but now they were used to reach the remote and backward regions of India. The media was support for Development communication. During the regime of Indira Gandhi, Television received a boost in India. In the year 1984-85, 120 transmitters were set up in India.

The liberalization policies of the early 1990s changed the media landscape, and the communication policies underwent a drastic change. Public broadcasters—All India Radio and Doordarshan had to generate their revenue. Private players entered the radio and television market. The entry of private players completely changed the focus of the media. The visuals of rural India disappeared from the media. The competition among private players to catch the eyeballs of the audience transformed the media into an entertainment medium.

The growing digitization in the 2000s has further changed the media landscape. The mobile handsets have revolutionized the production and consumption of media. The increasing internet penetration in the country and the emergence of OTT platforms have also added to the diversity in media and communication.

The Digital India idea of the Government of India seeks to connect, propel and secure universal broadband connectivity to all citizens of the country. In order to fulfil this objective, the National Digital Communication Policy 2018 has been drawn to replace the National Telecom Policy 2012. The key objectives are—broadband for all, creation of jobs in the communication sector, India among the top 50 nations in the ICT development Index of ITU and ensuring digital sovereignty.

The fourth industrial revolution has further widened the technological gap. At the normative level, freedom of speech and expression is a fundamental right. It is a social value that includes development and application of communication technology. In the current scenario, communication permeates education, health, economy, business, entertainment and all aspects of an individual's life. From the producer and delivery of communication point of view also wide diversity exists. A unified communication policy would help a balanced growth and coordinated functioning of the various parts.

References

Lee, John A.R. (1976). *Towards Realistic Communication Policies: Recent Trends and Ideas Compiled and Analysed*, UNESCO, Paris.

Mahesh Chandra Guru B.P. and Mariswamy H.K. (2014). *Globalisation and Communication Policy in India*, Concept Publishing Company, New Delhi.

Middleton John and Rahim Syed A. ed. (1977). Perspectives in Communication Policy and Planning, East-West Communication Institute, Hawaii

Virmani, Arvind (2000). "A Communication Policy for the 21st Century", *Economic and Political Weekly*, Vol. 35, No. 23.

Towards a National Policy on Communication in Support of Development:The Indian Case; unesdoc.unesco.org/ar/48223/pf0000034684

pib/gov.in/newsite/PrintRelease.aspx?relid=183711

1
Communication Policy in the Age of Facebook

Rohan Samarajiva

Introduction

It is a pleasure to be given this opportunity to reflect on communication policy, a subject I have taught and practiced in multiple countries over multiple decades. I have been fortunate to have entered the field at a time of rapid change and to have been able to witness the changes and, in some little ways, to contribute to them.

I will quickly place today's communication policy-making activities in historical context and move on to address the challenges, both operational and theoretical. I illustrate the challenges using examples from our region, including the recent zero-rating controversy.

Historical Context

National Communication Policy gained high profile in the 1970s (Rahim, 1977; Samarajiva, 1984) in a very different political and economic environment than what exists at present. This was when the European theatres of the Cold War had stabilized and the areas of contestation had shifted to the developing world. The optimism that we now experience because reforms in China and India have moved millions out of poverty and enriched many in their middle classes was then absent. It was a much bleaker time.

Then, the dividing line in the debate was about whether the state had any role as a provider of communication services. Opponents of UNESCO's promotion of national communication policy saw any discussion of a role for the state in communication policy as a stalking horse for state control and censorship. The proponents saw an urgent need for action outside the market to promote development and to compensate for market imperfections. Both saw national communication policy as necessarily involving a role for the state as an actor in the communication industry (Beltran S., 1977).

This was a reflection of broader economic debates that culminated in proposals for the New International Economic Order, drawing heavily from the thinking of Raul Prebisch (1950). Having seen the surge of economic growth in the Soviet Union under central planning, and influenced by Fabian thinking that saw a need for the state to control the "commanding heights" of the economy, nationalization of private enterprises and establishment of state-owned enterprises were popular those days. If the state had to control the commanding heights of the economy, should it also not control the commanding heights of society? Government-owned steel mills and nationalized banks were not producing the promised results and were in many cases creating additional problems. One explanation was that these policies were wrong. For those who did not want to accept that explanation, there were others.

One possible explanation was that the fault was in the people. They were not working hard enough; they were not committed enough to the cause of national development, they were unappreciative of the need for order and stability, and so on. This was because of the institutions that shaped their thinking, including the media. If the media could be compelled to do a better job, the people would behave better. A "new man" would produce a developed economy. Intermingled with this were other concerns, such as the difficulties of maintaining political power and/or stability and irritations about how Western media covered events in developing countries. Intended or not, the state was positioned as the central actor. Inadequate attention was paid to fundamental problems of the state in developing economies (Samarajiva, 1987).

National Policies Today

Today, there is little evidence of opposition to national policy *per se*. There are, of course, significant disagreements about what the content of national policies should be and how they should be implemented. And there is wide variation on the quality and comprehensiveness of policies and their implementation.

Almost all developed market economies periodically adopt communication policies or strategies, one of the most recent being by the UK Department of Culture, Media and Sports (2017). The purpose of these documents, variously described as policies, strategies and roadmaps, is that of providing a degree of certainty to the many actors active in the communication space. In the ideal case, such policies are broadly consulted and have the buy-in of most, if not all, government and non-government stakeholders. Having been approved by government through Cabinet or a similar superior committee and thus being difficult to change, there is a degree of rigidity to these policies which provide certainty to actors, especially to investors. Generally, these documents have to be complemented by more specific plans that set out targets, identify resources and assign responsibilities for the completion of tasks.

In India, especially in the Central Government, telecom policies tend to be developed through consultative processes and are taken seriously. It is often possible to establish causal relationships between what happens in the sector and what is written in the policy (Kathuria, 2000). For example, the new telecom policy of the Government of India (1999) converted the unviable payment structure imposed on mobile operators when originally licensed, into a royalty-based scheme. This made a significant contribution to the subsequent efflorescence of mobile telecommunications in India. On the other hand, the track record in broadcasting policy has been poor (Kumar, 2003; Kumar, 2007). Despite the floating of many drafts, a national policy has not been finalized and efforts to create an independent regulatory authority have been still born.

In other countries such as Bangladesh, Nepal and Sri Lanka, policy formulation and implementation is weak. The last proper national telecom policy in Bangladesh dates back to 1998, and in Sri Lanka to 1994. Nepal adopted both a National ICT Policy and a

Broadband Policy in 2015, but examination of earlier drafts (Government of Nepal, n.d.) showed that they were more in the nature of wish lists than actionable and resourced policies.

The Bangladesh and Sri Lanka policies were threadbare and had become obsolete long ago. Efforts to replace them with more modern documents have failed to go the distance, though some kind of policy appears to have been slapped together in Bangladesh (Daily Star, 2016), while the old policy is what is still displayed on government websites. However, the lack of formal policies does not appear to have caused serious damage to the sectors, which have kept growing and innovating. Of course, the question of whether they would have done even better if good policies were in place and were scrupulously implemented remains open (Samarajiva, 2008).

Challenges for Policy Formulation in the Communication Space

Operational

The practical aspects of formulating and implementing policy in the communication space have become increasingly challenging. In the old days, the scope or coverage of policy was narrow. Print media were distinct and separate from electronic media. Telecommunications were not even seen as having a connection with media, except in the USA and Canada where privately owned long-distance transmission facilities carried both voice communication and the content of network radio and television systems. A single Ministry used to be able to make and implement policy with a defined scope.

In recent decades, convergence on a scale that was difficult to envisage in the 1970s has occurred. Television supplanted newspapers as the primary source of news, only to be overtaken by social media, at least in developed market economies and even in some developing ones. Television programmes are being watched not only on desktop and laptop computers, but even on the small screens of smartphones. In countries where cable was the primary means of gaining access to television content, cable is surviving only in instances where they successfully made the transition to delivering fast Internet access.

Main stream media (MSM) and new media compete for the finite amounts of attention that are available. As television gained attention, newspapers lost readers. By 2016, 62 per cent of US adults obtained news on social media, and 18 per cent did so often, according to a survey by Pew Research Center, conducted in association with the John S. and James L. Knight Foundation (Gottfried & Shearer, 2016). In the final analysis, media convergence is less about the same "pipes" being used and more about the same attention being sought by different media.

The shift may be illustrated also with data from Sri Lanka, a backward country in terms of new media. A recent report by the Secretariat for Media Reforms (2016) reports that advertising outlays (LKR 1 billion or INR 500 million, and growing) already being spent on new media in Sri Lanka as opposed to around LKR 30 billion (or INR 15 billion) on all advertising. Mobile phones are now the most common electronic device in homes, followed by TV and radios. Most people access the Internet over mobile devices.

A representative-sample survey of media consumption in the Western Province (with 42% of the economy and around 30% of the population of Sri Lanka) released by the Centre for Policy Alternatives (2016) found that "private television is the most popular source of news for the respondents, followed by Facebook and the Internet/Web. When breaking down the findings by age category, Facebook is the main source of news for the 18-24 year respondents followed by private television stations and the Internet/Web."

The Western Province is not Sri Lanka and 18-24 year olds are not the entirety of the population. But as the leading province, it is the best available guide to the future trajectory of media development in the country. MSM are already losing the attention of a key demographic. As this demographic ages, they will take with them the habits and preferences formed as they became adults. The subsequent cohorts will not revert to MSM. Advertising rupees will follow attention. MSM in the current form will shrivel and die. The few that succeed in becoming trusted content providers on new-media platforms will survive.

In Myanmar, until recently at the bottom of ICT performance indicator tables but is now in the midst of rapid growth, LIRNEasia (2016) research showed that in mid-2016, 83 per cent of households had a mobile phone, more than TV (61%) and radio (16%). Of those who owned phones, 78 per cent owned smartphones, a percentage in the same range as in the United States. Among owners, 49 per cent used data services and 35 per cent used Facebook. Twenty one per cent of phone owners used Facebook everyday. In 2016, TV and radio were given as the primary source of information by 9 per cent and 4 per cent, respectively, of those in 15-65 age group. Internet was the primary source of information for 9 per cent and calls over mobile for 15 per cent. Newspapers were negligible.

So it would not make much sense now to come up with different policies for television, radio, newspapers etc. paying no heed to new media. But bringing new media, with their user-generated content and algorithms for prioritizing what the users see would require stretching the conventional capabilities of media ministries and their experts.

A communication policy that does not include a section on security, would now be considered incomplete.[1] Communication regulators have begun to address the terms and conditions of interconnection between different mobile financial services, a topic that is normally within the remit of financial regulators (Jaindi, 2017).

Not only does ICT policy have to cover hitherto distinct subjects such as telecom, Internet, radio and TV, but it also has to address what is done over the electronic platforms. For example, the UK Digital Strategy includes actions and commitments related to healthcare delivery such as electronic patient records, apps and wearable devices, telehealth and assistive technologies.[2]

What all this means is that it has become very difficult to develop and implement a coherent communication policy under a single ministry as in the past.

Theoretical

Though difficult, it is possible to develop a comprehensive, modern policy for the communication space through diligent consultation and the involvement of multiple agencies of government. But it would suffer from a fundamental instability. This is because the media (broadly defined) are no longer just a segment of the economy. They are at the core of the economy. It is difficult to define the bounds of communication policy, which keep shifting and expanding. This is the underlying cause of the operational difficulties.

The business model pioneered in newspapers by Pulitzer in the waning years of the 19th Century migrated to the Internet *via* television and radio. The essence of this business model was the aggregation and sale of attention, in the form of audiences. The evidence of its rise was the decreasing proportion of revenue derived from direct payments by subscribers by a supplier of media content such as a newspaper or magazine. With private radio and television channels, the price to a consumer went down to zero. Over this period, the "attention economy" became established and understood.

Nobel Laureate Herbert Simon (1971) first described the attention economy: "Hence a wealth of information creates a poverty of attention and a need to allocate that attention efficiently among the overabundance of information sources that might consume it." What this means is that the most scarce, and therefore, most valuable, commodity today is attention.

Attention is the precondition for the occurrence of a transaction (an exchange of value) and, thereby, of economic relationships (iterated transactions). Not all aggregations of attention (audiences) are markets, but all markets require the assembly of attention (production of audiences). In the marketing literature, the term "prospect" is used to describe a person likely to become a customer. Prospects are better described as audiences, because attention is central to the success of conversion to customer (Samarajiva, 1997, p. 286).

Contrary to expectations by 1980s thinking exemplified by the title of a book by Mosco (1989) "pay-per society", the dominant business model for ICT-centric enterprises has been the extension of what first emerged in mass media: give away content below cost and monetize the attention. Expectations of the replacement of flat-rate or free models by use-based pricing were created by the ability of emerging systems to measure use at negligible cost and the resulting reduction of transaction costs of billing. But as Hotmail, Google and Facebook demonstrated, free was a price that was difficult to beat.

It was true that the new ICT-centric enterprises collected data on use at negligible cost. But this was not for the purpose of "metered use" as expected by Mosco *et al.* It was to produce meta-audiences, meso-audience and audiences (Samarajiva, 1997, p. 287):

> An *audience* is defined as persons attending to a specific message. This [definition] stays close to the core meaning of an audience as an auditory collective... The audience does not have to be in the same place or be paying attention at the same time. Those attending to a message need not reach a common understanding, nor does attention have to be efficacious from the communicator's perspective.
>
> A *meso-audience* is defined as persons likely to attend to a class of messages. A "daypart," a term of art from the television industry, is an example. There is no presumption that all those within a meso-audience will end up in the audiences intended.... The more effective the process of producing a meso-audience is, the greater the probability of that outcome.....
>
> A *meta-audience* is defined as that from which meso-audiences and audiences may be produced. Uses such as "the audience for Channel 6" or the "television audience" would fall within this definition. Subscribers to the Internet would be another example....

The case of zero rating illustrates the value of these theoretical distinctions. It was a highly controversial policy issue in India, which involved mobile operators, Internet companies, e-commerce providers and even newspaper companies. The Telecom Authority of India (TRAI) consultations attracted in excess of one million submissions.

Zero-rated data are data that are not counter toward the user's quota under the data cap. When a specific application or content is zero-rated, the user may consume an unlimited amount of that specific content without incurring data charges (Galpaya, 2017 : 2). One reason for the incoherence of regulatory decisions (evidenced by TRAI having to revisit the topic repeatedly) is the inability to understand the economic basis of zero rating and the incentives of the key players.

Galpaya (2017 : 3) states that "zero-rated data provision is [not] costless... Some other entity in the Internet value chain bears the costs. Usually, it is the MNO [mobile network operator] or the OTT player [Internet company] (or both) who bears them. The cost of the user's bandwidth to access the zero-rated content is borne by the MNO, or paid to the MNO by the OTT player, or shared between the MNO and OTT player, depending on how the specific business model is structured."

The interests of mobile operators and Internet companies such as Facebook diverge on many issues such as taxation, lawful interception etc. In the case of zero rating, their interests are aligned, both preferring to work out the zero-rated offers between themselves without regulation. It is well-known that mobile operators see Internet companies as long-term existential threats.

For many, the offering of zero-rated content by mobile operators is understandable as part of a strategy to convert voice-only customers to voice-and-data customers by giving away some attractive content (but leaving some desirable content just beyond their reach) or zero-rating specific content for a limited introductory periods. Beyond the give-away is the prospect of greater revenues. By increasing the number of data users on their networks, the mobile operators also increase the attractiveness of the meta-audience they produce. In a competitive environment, that larger the meta-audience, or the higher-quality the meta-audience (having more purchasing power or similar characteristics that may be described through data analytics), the greater the negotiating power the mobile operator will have *vis-à-vis* producers of meso-audiences or audiences.

But understanding the motivation of Internet companies that do not get any payments from the users of their services is a greater challenge. The only revenues that come to the Internet companies are from advertisers. At the present time, Facebook and other Internet companies may be seen as producers of meso-audiences. They can describe the meso-audiences in much greater detail than can the mobile operators and can offer raw material for the production of audiences unlimited by national boundaries. Because the content that attracts the meso-audience as well as the data are contributed by the users themselves, the costs of producing the meso-audience are low. As a result, they are making money hand over fist.

Mobile operators and Internet companies are adversarial because of signs that the Internet companies may not be content to limit their activities to the production of meso-audiences but may be reaching down to the level of meta-audiences through their experimentation with fibre to the home (now discontinued by Google), balloons floating 18 km above the ground (GoogleX's Loon), and drones (Facebook) and less directly through investments in undersea cables and interventions in spectrum auctions. Seeing the revenues being earned by the producers of meso-audiences, telecom operators are also making efforts to enter that level, as evidenced by the recent roll-back of restrictions on data collection by telecom operators by the Federal Communications Commission (FCC) in the United States (Kang, 2017).

But the key point is not simply that attention is shifting from one medium to another. It is that attention is becoming central to the functioning of industries beyond MSM. This is what is happening with e-commerce businesses such as Myntra and Amazon and even with taxi ordering platforms such as Uber. In the same way that Pulitzer gave away his newspaper for less than the cost of producing it, e-commerce companies are giving away their services for less than cost of production. Those still thinking with old categories call it "capital dumping" (Sehgal, 2017), an inane term if there was one.

But, if one steps back, it is possible to see that the services are being subsidized in order to establish the largest possible base of customers with loyalty to the company which is sought to be ensured by heavy advertising and data analytics. Through apps and various other means, the old search for prospects is being transformed to a contest for audiences. The art of holding customers is still a work in progress, so success is not guaranteed.

Conclusion

The communication space has been transformed by the attention economy. Thinking on policy has changed, with policy expected to set the ground rules for all participants rather than just define the role of the state. Operational challenges are significant given the difficulties of delimiting the scope of communication policy. But even more challenging is that theory has not caught up with practice. What is now being done is akin to driving, looking in the rearview mirror (McLuhan & Parker, 1989). It is when policy is informed by theory that accurately reflects the world as it exists that we are likely to see practically adequate policy.

Notes

1. https://www.gov.uk/government/publications/uk-digital-strategy/5-a-safe-and-secure-cyberspace-making-the-uk-the-safest-place-in-the-world-to-live-and-work-online
2. https://www.gov.uk/government/publications/uk-digital-strategy/summary-and-annex

References

Beltran S., L.R. (1977). National communication policies in Latin America: A glance at the first steps, In *Perspectives in communication policy and planning*, eds. Rahim, S.A. and Middleton, J. (pp. 185-233). Honolulu HI: East West Center.

Centre for Policy Alternatives (2016). Consumption and perceptions of mainstream and social media in the Western Province. http://www.cpalanka.org/full-report-consumption-and-perceptions-of-mainstream-and-social-media-in-the-western-province/

Daily Star (2016, June 28). New telecom policy finally gets nod, *Daily Star*. http://www.thedailystar.net/business/new-telecom-policy-finally-gets-nod-1246846

Galpaya, H. (2017, February 23). *Zero rating in emerging economies*. Paper Series No. 47. Global Commission on Internet Governance. https://www.ourinternet.org/sites/default/files/publications/GCIG%20no.47_1.pdf

Gottfried, J.; Shearer, E. (2016, May 26). News use across social media platforms 2016, http://www.journalism.org/2016/05/26/news-use-across-social-media-platforms-2016/

Government of India (1999). New telecom policy. http://www.trai.gov.in/about-us/acts-policies/new-telecom-policy-1999

Government of Nepal (n.d.). Draft National Broadband Policy. http://www.nta.gov.np/ne/component/joomdoc/Broadband%20Policy-Draft.pdf/download

Jaindi, K. (2017, February 23). Safaricom faces M-Pesa break up in market dominance war, *Daily Nation*. http://www.nation.co.ke/business/Safaricom-faces-M-Pesa-break-up-in-market-dominance-war-/996-3824618-vdv5gw/index.html

Kang, C. (2017, March 1). F.C.C., in potential sign of the future, halts new data security rules, *New York Times*, https://www.nytimes.com/2017/03/01/technology/fcc-data-security-rules.html?emc=edit_tu_20170310&nl=bits&nlid=9770121&te=1&_r=0

Kathuria, R. (2000). Telecom policy reforms in India, *Global Business Review*, *1*(2).

Kumar, Kanchan (2003). Mixed signals: Radio broadcasting policy in India. *Economic and Political Weekly*, *38*(22): 2173-2182.

Kumar, Keval J. (2007). Media education, regulation and public policy in India. www.diplomatie.gouv.fr/fr/IMG/pdf/KevalKumar.pdf

LIRNEasia (2016). Mobile phones, Internet, information, knowledge: Myanmar 2016. http://lirneasia.net/2017/01/ict-use-in-myanmar-2016-survey-results-present-to-deputy-minister/

McLuhan, M. and Parker, H. (1968). *Through the Vanishing Point: Space in Poetry and Painting*. New York: Harper and Row, London: Evanston.

Mosco, V. (1989). *The pay-per society: Computers and communication in the information age*. Norwood NJ: Ablex.

Prebisch, R. (1950). *The economic development of Latin America and its principal problems*. New York: UN Department of Economic Affairs.

Rahim, S.A. (1977). Introduction: The scope of communication policy and planning research, in *Perspectives in communication policy and planning*, eds. Rahim, S.A. and Middleton, J. (pp. 5-24). Honolulu HI: East West Center.

Samarajiva, R. (1984). The history of the New Information Order. *Journal of Communication*, *34*(4): 110-115.

Samarajiva, R. (1987). Le nouvel ordre de l'information: Retrospective et prospective. *Revue Tiers-Monde*, *28*(3): 677-678.

Samarajiva, R. (1997). Interactivity as though privacy mattered, in Agre, P. and Rotenberg, M. (eds) *Technology and privacy: The new landscape* (pp. 277-309). Cambridge MA: MIT Press.

Samarajiva, R. (2008), Introduction, in Samarajiva, R.; Zainudeen, A. eds. *ICT infrastructure in emerging Asia: Policy and regulatory roadblocks*. New Delhi and Ottawa: Sage & IDRC. https://www.idrc.ca/en/book/ict-infrastructure-emerging-asia-policy-and-regulatory-roadblocks

Secretariat for Media Reforms (2016). *Rebuilding public trust: An assessment of the media industry and profession in Sri Lanka*. Colombo: SMR/IMS. https://www.mediasupport.org/publication/rebuilding-public-trust-assessment-media-industry-profession-sri-lanka/

Sehgal, K. (2017, January 31). Indian VC Mahesh Murthy rips apart 'hollow arguments' of Vani Kola on 'capital dumping.' *Techseen*. http://techseen.com/2017/01/31/mahesh-murthy-vani-kola-spar-capital-dumping/

Simon, H.A. (1971). Designing organizations for an information-rich world, in Greenberger, M. *Computers, communication, and the public interest* (pp. 40-41). Baltimore. MD: The Johns Hopkins Press.

UK Department of Culture, Media and Sport (2017). *UK digital strategy: A policy paper.* https://www.gov.uk/government/publications/uk-digital-strategy

2

Media and Communication Policy Need for Children in India

A Historical Analysis in Search of a Fresh Paradigm

Binod C. Agrawal

Introduction

The reason to be here today is my serious concern for children and rural cultivators over four decades. This concern has changed my professional career from Anthropology to Satellite Communication. Since 1973, I have been involved in studying effects or impact of Television on the Indian child and the cultivators (Agrawal, 1978). The Indian child has become my preoccupation and continues to be one of the most important media and communication research concern (Agrawal, 1997a, 1997b and 1997c).

Hence, most of my comments and observations on the issues related to media and communication policy for children in India are derived from my earlier studies and observations (Agrawal, 2009). Attempt has been made to give a historical perspective to bring out learning from first hand deliberation and participation in several national media and communication policy committees from time to time.

Context

In mid-seventies of last century, as a part of social evaluation of world's largest techno-social experiment, the Satellite Instructional Television Experiment (SITE) was carried out for one year during 1975-76 in India. SITE covered 2,400 villages equally divided among six economically backward States and more than 400 villages of Kheda District, Gujarat. Both qualitative and quantitative village studies were carried out to assess the social effect or impact of SITE in all seven States. These studies clearly indicated that in SITE villages, a large majority of Television viewers were children from almost all socio-economic households.

Before SITE, these children would have spent their time in playing on the hard and rough ground and often would have looked to the sky to express their helplessness and to seek help. Largely, majority of these children belonged to the poor landless households referred to as "below poverty line" by the State administration. A very small number of these young children from affluent and well to do households would have grown up in the laps tugged in human warmth while looking down upon their poor and unfortunate brethren. The parents of these children owned large chunks of agricultural land and commanded power and respect in the village and grew up in a highly "class" bound social hierarchy of *Garib* (poor) and *Amir* (rich) (Agrawal, 1978).

Changing Communication and Media Scenario

Communication revolution has touched almost every life in India within forty years. Earlier, I had observed that Television viewing among children was growing very rapidly unabated. The process has accelerated since then, that too of all forms of digital media (Anonymous, 2015). Television has recorded unprecedented expansion after invasion of international Television network for children in several Indian languages apart from original American, Australian, British, English. So, today children are one of the largest Television consumers (viewers) both in rural and urban areas more than Radio and print media (Agrawal, 2017).

Today's child has become an international issue for debate in the market place as media 'consumer' and as 'producer'. Should media and communication policy for children be treated exclusively as a national or global issue? The media and communication policy, if viewed in a global perspective, the chances are that, the cultural specificity of the policy will be diluted and lost. At the same time, if examined within the national context, the socio-cultural factors specific and unique to Indian civilization would take precedence. I tend to accept the contextual view and like to consider and propose media and communication policy for children within the socio-cultural context of democratic India.

In democratic India, media and communication policy has been widely debated since the days of the Constituent Assembly in 1948. The Parliament, the Supreme Court and print media have generated political controversies and inconclusive discussions. Ideological positions have been taken on media and communication policy among intellectuals, elites, politicians, bureaucrats and the public at large that included adolescents and school going children. While there is a general consensus to have a sound and workable communication and media policy suited to India, it remained elusive and sporadic. Often efforts have been made in response to fulfil political demands in which children were totally forgotten.

Colonial Legacy and After

Commerce and business was the motto of British colonial masters who formulated communication and media policy using the prism of profit and loss. So, they created a clear media and communication dichotomy between "public" and "private" media and communication ownership, distribution and production leaving the entire creative and cultural communication expressions out of the preview of any policy discussion (Edwardes, 1967 [2011]). The colonial legacy continued until 1992 by default in Independent India. No systemic policy effort was made, during all these years, to have broad view of the media and communication policy to cope with the reconstruction, revival and revitalization of the ancient civilization of India to adapt, adopt and integrate various forms of communication and theme in the democratic governance. Also no new ways of administration came forward that would require democratic media and communication policy with special focus on children.

The policy-makers in India have yet to find time to formulate an appropriate media and communication policy for children. Though they have recognized the importance of an independent press and electronic media since first Prime Minister Jawaharlal Nehru felt that the people of India were not ready to have free press and radio leave aside telecommunications. Often Nehru's successors reiterated the same view on the floor of the Indian Parliament.

The result is an improvised mixed bag of outdated approach of colonial control for media and communication policy. There is little progress in the democratic policy that lacks well-defined media and communication policy for children. Another problem of media and communication policy in India is that digital media, Film, Television, Radio, Print, ancient creative and cultural expressions (treated as folk media) and telecommunications are categorized separately as a colonial hangover.

Hence, the term 'communication' is used to denote telecommunications; 'media' is used to denote radio and television; 'press' for print media; while 'film' is a separate category. Folk media denote and include varieties of several millennia old socio-religious music, drama and theatre popular performances across length and breadth of the country. Innumerable oral means of communications, "musical traditions" and "art and dance forms" find scanty space in the media and communication policy formulation. The policy is largely based on the colonial categories thought to be accurate depictions and descriptions of plural and multi layered cultural realities of the Indian civilization.

There has been evolution of multiple policy formulations within the confines of limited cultural, linguistic and social understanding of the Indian civilization. So, it has led to the emergence of several overlapping often contradictory media and communication policies, each treating only a part of the whole. In the process, the recognition of linguistic and cultural specificity and plurality as well as communication interdependence and interrelationships among the media men and women and children have been left untouched (Agrawal and Sinha eds., 1986; Thakur and Agrawal eds., 1989 [2004]). Further fragmentation in defining media and communication policy has taken place as a result of various pressure groups demanding specific policies to safeguard their interest and rights. Demands for separate media policies for children, women, minorities and weaker sections, to mention a few have additionally complicated the issue of an integrated media and communication policy. These demands overlook the problems of multilayered cultural plurality, status, and position of children in the family and gender linked differences in the socialization process. These factors need immediate attention and action to create equality between genders.

Satellite Era

The advent of satellite communication, transnational electronic printing facility, methods of information transfer through electronic mail, virtual world of digital media, superhighway, and convergence of communication technologies have further complicated the existing media and communication policy which is already somewhat outdated and redundant in India and in many parts of the world.

Methods of media control by government are becoming obsolete as a result of the onslaught of digital media adoption and use (Anonymous, 2015). The question then arises: What kind of media and communication policy should be formulated for the smooth and democratic governance of all that could be conducive and culturally compatible for the wholesome development of the child? Current policies, it seems, have indifferent or "anti-child" bias though some serious efforts are afoot towards 'girl child' also reflecting paternalistic age old prejudices and colonial legacy in absence of any clear "pro-people" and "pro-children" media and communication policy.

The time has come to examine, discuss and debate the socio-cultural and political assumptions being made in the formulation of media and communication policy, to save the children from possible adverse anti-democratic and conflicting cultural influences of media so they do not grow as maladjusted future generation of men and women. Such a perspective will allow better understanding of the children in the formulation of media and communication policy for children and will show the path of future directions in democratic India (Gupta and Dyal, 1996).

Plural Culture and Media Policy for Children: A Proposal

The policy-makers and Government of India have treated India as a single coherent civilization while discussing any policy including media and communication policy. Several commissions and committees set up by the Government of India reinforced such a view to bring about cultural uniformity and to incorporate the marginalized people into the national mainstream thereby ignoring the existence of cultural plurality. Volumes of reports of various working groups, committees and commissions set up by the Government of India on media and communication policy and child related issues have accumulated dust without any real change as a British colonial legacy (Yadava, 1985).

Since India's Independence until internal emergency declared in 1975, All-India Radio and Television were under complete government control and protection with limited coverage, in absence of media policy and due to lack of public scrutiny. The closest to a plausible media policy can be found in pronouncements on the rationale for the introduction of Television in 1959. The first Committee Report on Information and Broadcasting Ministry (1966) focused on 'School Education' and not on the child though more than two-third children were out of school in those years.

During the dark days of internal emergency (1975-77) in India, the media became an important and exclusive tool for the government's propaganda, policy pronouncements and political personal glorification. After emergency was lifted, demands were made for full autonomy of electronic media and the restructuring of media and communication policy. Akash Bharati Bill, 1978, was introduced in the Parliament which provided "for the establishment of a national broadcast trust called *Akash Bharati* as an autonomous and independent public service to conduct, organize, regulate, license and develop all forms of broadcasting in India and for all matters connected therewith or incidental thereto." (Akash Bharati: 1978:207). Akash Bharati (1978:227) took upon itself the responsibility "to protect the interest of children, the blind, and the aged and other vulnerable section of the population". However, there was no elaboration as to how the same could be achieved.

Another Working Group for 'Planning of Software' was set up in 1982. One of the members of the Working Group was a child development expert. She insisted that children must be considered as a separate target group to take advantage of Television for their social and emotional development. So, a full chapter in the report was devoted to children entitled "Children: Victims or Beneficiaries" and it discussed a whole range of topics to be covered to improve the production quality of children's programmes. The report observed:

> For some children, Television programmes may help to supplement what has already been learnt at school. A vast section of our child population, however, has little or no access to educational facilities. For these children, Television can serve a particularly important function. It can help not just to develop their literacy skills, but can also stimulate their intellectual development by exposing them to a wide range of new situations, events and ideas. Television can help in fostering the development of desirable values and habits among children. (An Indian Personality for Television, 1985:39). It appears that the Government has shifted the focus of media and communication policy from control to regulate without explicit power to formulate policies for strengthening Indian democracy and wholesome development of the children.

So far, media and communication policy in the country has yet to find an integrated and holistic expression. It is because policies have been drawn from time to time for each medium. Further these policies have tried to accommodate expressions of minorities, disadvantaged, women, children and others. Hence, it is proposed that a media and communication policy for children must form a sub-set of an integrated and holistic media policy that incorporates specificities of plurality of the Indian civilization. Also in the policy a well-defined statement must be incorporated on the role of government as regulator rather than controller. So equal opportunity is ensured for the communication of child rights in the light of similar regulations elsewhere in the world (Unnikrishnan and Bajpai, 1996).

References

Agrawal, Binod C. (1978). *Television Comes to Village: An Evaluative Study of SITE*. Bangalore: Indian Space Research Organisation.

—— (1997a). The Meaning of Hinglishness: Liberalisation and Globalisation in Indian Broadcasting. *In* United Nations World Television Forum. ed., Kevin Robins, pp. 144-155. RAI Report.

—— (1997b). Television Policy in India: Future Directions presented during "AMIC-India National Conference on Television: Beyond 2000" held at Chennai, November 14-15, 1997.

—— (1997c). Media Policy for Children in India: Is There a Need ? Keynote address at the Seminar on *'Towards a Media Policy for Children"* held at SNDT College of Home Science, Pune, 26-28 December, 1997.

—— (2009). *Television in the life of Child in India: Some observations*. Invited talk at State Institute of Educational Technology, Lucknow (UP), February 13, 2009.

—— (2010). An Unfinished Saga of Basic E Support Television (BEST): Methods of Pre- and Post-Script Testing. Paper Presented in the National Consultative Meeting NCERT, New Delhi, May 6-7, 2010 (in association with Mira Aghi and Rukmini Vemraju).

—— (2014). Media and the Child in India. Chairpersons Remarks in the National Seminar on "Women and Children in Media: Issues and Perspective" held on March 26-27, 2014 at M.S. University Baroda, Vadodara.

—— (2017). *Digital Media for Sustainable Development: Future of Poor becoming Pauper in India*. Paper presented in 4th ICMC Conference held on January 10-12, 2017 at MICA, Ahemdabad, India.

Agrawal Binod C. and Mira B. Aghi (eds.) (1987). *Television and the Indian Child*. New Delhi: UNICEF.

Agrawal Binod C., and Arbind K. Sinha (eds.) (1986a). *Site to Insight: Challenge of Production and Research for Women and Children*. New Delhi: Concept Publishing Co.

Agrawal, Binod C. *et al.* (1987). *Situational Analysis of Children's Television in India*. New Delhi: Concept Publishing Co.

Anonymous (2015). *KAP Study Integrated Report for Developing Communication Plans Under Swachh Bharat Mission in Four Districts of Madhya Pradesh*. Ahmedabad: TALEEM Research Foundation (Project Leader Binod C. Agrawal).

The Broadcasting Bill (1997). The Broadcasting, Bill No. 71 of 1997 to be introduced in Lok Sabha. New Delhi: Government of India.

Doordarshan (1997). New Delhi: Audience Research Unit, Directorate General Doordarshan.

Edwardes, Michael (1967). British India 1772-1947. New Delhi: Rupa & Co (sixth Impression 2011).

Gupta, V.S. and Rajeshwar Dyal (eds.) (1996). National Media Policy. Ministry of Information and Broadcasting, New Delhi: Concept Publishing Company.

Gupta, V.S. and Rajeshwar Dyal (eds.) (1985). *An Indian Personality for Television*, Vol. 1 and 2: Report of the Working Group on Software for Doordarshan. New Delhi: Publications Division, Ministry of Information and Broadcasting.

Akash Bharati (1978). *Akash Bharati National Broadcast Trust: Report of the Working Group on Autonomy for Akashvani and Doordarshan.* New Delhi: Ministry of Information and Broadcasting, Government of India.

—— (1966). *Committee Report on Information and Broadcasting Media.* New Delhi: Publication Division, Ministry of Information and Broadcasting.

Thakur, B.S. and Binod C. Agrawal (eds.) (1989). *Media Utilisation for the Development of Women and Children.* New Delhi: Concept Publishing Company.

Unnikrishnan, Narula and Shailaja Bajpai (1996). *The Impact of Television Advertising on Children.* New Delhi: Sage Publication.

Yadava, Jaswant S. (1985). *Policies of News: Third World Perspectives.* New Delhi: Concept Publishing Company.

3

Is a Comprehensive Communication Policy for India Possible

Buroshiva Dasgupta

A 'comprehensive' communication strategy for country's development which is planned by the government, will certainly have to look into not just how to make best use of the new media technologies, which includes the satellite, the internet and the mobile. All these new media technologies lay down guidelines for the content. The task would be controversial—to say the least.

With the new social media becoming the thrust area for policy research, has its own implications for individuals as well as for the institutions. Organizations like the Prasar Bharati (which regulates television and radio) appears less comprehensive, while the Press Council (for the print media) has long been accused of being 'toothless'. TRAI, since inception, has been restricted to the technical strategies of the country's telecommunication revolution and has hardly any say in 'content' making.

The government proposes to link the new communication policy with the country's development strategies and finalise a draft, after a detailed discussion with the states's views of professional communicators are important for a comprehensive document on communication for development. For the sake of federalism, the document cannot be drawn up entirely by the bureaucrats of the centre and the states. The media is accused—and sometimes justifiably so

— of being biased and restrictive. The media, it is said, hardly covers 'development' news. But no policy on communication can be thrust on the media without an open discussion. There is enough sanity left in the media even now to tap into.

How do you ensure the constitutional mandate of "freedom of speech"? The Twitter is not just PMO's handle for propaganda nor the radio exclusive for "Man ki Baat". A 'comprehensives' strategy needs to be drawn up in a way where government propaganda and free speech can exist side by side.

Let us take up a concrete example of a strategic communication plan for development successfully implemented in a neighbouring country. In Bangladesh, for example, UNICEF has drawn up a guidebook for communication strategies for development. It suggests a few common 'conceptual models'—like ACADA (Assessment, Communication Analysis, Design and Action), the 5-point Process (Analysis, Design, Testing, Implementation and Evaluation), and COMBI (Communication for Behavioural Impact)—for developing a strategic communication plan for the country's development.

One must admit that Bangladesh, by implementing these strategic communication plans, has improved the country's health conditions vastly in the last few years. Though the country has a lower GDP growth rate than India, it now occupies a higher position than India in world's Human Development Index (HDI) ladder of the governments. Media has to rework on its focus. But, the important question is: Is development journalism meant to be government propaganda? N. Ram, Editor in Chief of the *Hindu*, in a lecture in Kolkata sometime ago, mentions certain 'trends' in the media—like 'paid' news, 'misleading' news, 'hyper-dependence' on advertising (he says 85 per cent of media revenue comes from advertising)— are leading the media to a crisis which might lead to 'external' regulation. Ram strongly recommends 'self-correction'. He does not find much sense in appointing a retired judge as an external ombudsman (as *Times of India* does) because he thinks he has not much to do but suggest a fulltime appointment as a 'reader's editor (or public editor) as the *Hindu* does, and who can be open to readers' suggestions and internally guard against plagiarism, paid news and similar misdeeds.

With the present trends continuing, Ram says, media is asking for trouble. Added to the trends pointed out by Ram, we now could add 'fake' news and 'trolling' of the social media. In that case, surely the media will be regulated from outside, by law, by the constitution, by judges, by others and as an editor, he adds, "I don't want that to happen".

On this note, Ram and many others like him in the media would object to a direct formulation of a national policy on communication if at all, as it is feared to affect the democratic potentials of the media. Certainly, there should be more vigorous internal discussions within the media and in the universities and research centres teaching media.

Some of the universities and colleges teaching media have held workshops and discussions on 'News Literacy'—a new global movement initiated by Stonybrook University to develop a strategy primarily to detect 'fake' news in the social media. This is again a welcome move—internal effort within the media fraternity (both among practitioners and academic).

The movement has also now involved Facebook and Google authorities to take up initiatives to devise ways to detect and eliminate fake news in circulation within the net. These internal efforts hopefully will reduce trolling and also avoid government clampdown and arbitrary blocking of sites.

Ram mentions the 'adversarial' role of the media which strengthens the democratic structure of the country. The critical, adversarial quality of media needs to stay. While more space to development stories needs to be given in the media, the government cannot expect the media to become its spokesperson.

A code of practice already exists for advertising, print, and broadcasting. Another may be drawn up for the fast growing social media but that too independent of government dictum. The government can be a facilitator, not the regulator of the media.

4

Behaviour Change of Youth in Bangladesh by the Use of Internet and Exposure to Foreign TV Channels

Golam Rahman

I wanted to learn the perceptions of the behaviour change from our youth and I have compiled two previous studies together. As you know that the democratic evidence show youth is a very high potential group of the nation in both Bangladesh, in India and many other countries. So this means about 18-35 years of age in our national policy for the youth development is called youth. It is a big range but it is going to be changed very soon also by 2050.

Our internet user is 66,965 million, day before yesterday by Bangladesh Telecommunication Regulatory Commission. They say it is increasing. With that it also increases their behavioural change due to internet. I also compiled from my previous study of satellite watching. Satellite television means the television other than our country's channels, particularly the foreign satellite television channels and also internet together. I want to say that the use of internet, the smartphones make real supplement to our behaviour.

Bangladesh has achieved the position among top 10 countries, providing mobile phones in numbers because we have got 165 billion people in our small country and number of mobile telephones is 84.95 per cent of our population but in India it is 87.99 per cent and in Pakistan it is 77 per cent.

My sample size was 332 among divisions of Dakha..., among the public and the private university and college students, youth. Their internet usage showed that about 70 per cent use internet everyday. That means 70 per cent of the youth sample use internet. I just push through some statistics like this. They are 56.3 per cent use at their home, in their laptop or in their computer and in mobile 26.5 per cent, among them largest users like 26.2 per cent use internet 8 hours in a week then 16 ours in a week about 23.2 per cent and more than 32 hours is 15 per cent so weekly users of 8 hours and more became 69 per cent of the sampled youth. So they use internet very much.

But for what they use? Major uses like Facebook 87 per cent, 37 per cent to watch video and 43 per cent also chat. But many of them say Facebook is also part of chatting. And also uploading or downloading of pictures 52 per cent and 58 per cent said that they use internet for their study. So these are major areas of uses that you see here.

Their perception of use is also important. What do they do? Increasing of knowledge, it was about 76 per cent and its major segment 61 per cent said they are using internet for the first time. For information and other services 49 per cent devote themselves. Among the users I asked personal questions like how do they maintain their confidentiality of using internet? 64 per cent said that they maintain their confidentiality and 89 per cent feel they are under surveillance. But 48 per cent say that will not bother about anything. Means the respondents will not bother while using internet.

Regarding their norms and freedom we asked questions like, do they enjoy to you. Less than half of the samples said they enjoy freedom. It is 45 per cent. And respondents have to oblige to societal norms agreed upon. And 67 per cent think that they should oblige the social norms, values of the society. And this is very important for them. And among their behaviour, their activities I found some interesting perceptions that about 31 per cent like to buy fast food and about 53 per cent use moderately and they are fond of fast food. But, 13 per cent do not like. so very small segment said they do not like fast food. Similarly, regarding soft drink 39 per cent said they like very much and moderately about 50 per cent and only 9 per cent said they do not like soft drink.

And when they were asked about companion of shopping whether they want to bring their friends or family members. Then 58 per cent said that Friends Company is important while shopping and 25 per cent said family and others a small segment. When they were asked whether their internet has got a role to build their life or career or future, 62 per cent thought internet has role to play so they are very optimistic and positive to use internet. Again when they were asked very psychologically whether just because of internet any of his friends got spoiled of deviated in their behaviour? 27 per cent agreed on that. 45 per cent said No. 23 per cent said they do not think anything. So this is a question I proposed because what about the image of internet that they should think of. Is it a tool or is it also something else than that. So just to understand the real situation among the youth we tried to post this question. Again we wanted to maintain present status that they are happy, sober and good. Every year 88.6 per cent said they wanted to maintain present status and 72 per cent wanted to be prominent in life and about 49 per cent wanted to be good in profession. So these are all their personal perceptions.

When we asked whether internet should be more open or more controlled. 2 per cent said internet is a necessity. 42 per cent said influence of internet is inevitable. 49 per cent said internet should be treated more open. So the youth thought in that line. And only 16.3 per cent negative influence. 35.5 per cent did not think anything at all. Respondent perceives the world of internet. May be these are the similar way of perception. At the same time 68.8 per cent want to own a family, want to stay with parents, their family values, social values very positive still. Regarding positive behaviour by social development to take place by communication is positive is 74 per cent. In a way those are positive values they are maintaining.

And another study that is satellite TV watching on foreign language, Hindi in Bangladesh or English, with 443 samples of 20 different occupational groups. We found their change in thinking, expectations, behaviour and lifestyle as a result to the exposure of satellite television programmes. 23 per cent of them had interest in uttering English word, around 9 per cent tried to use Hindi word while talking. 16 per cent mentioned their changing of dress options, their clothing and 12 per cent imitation hairstyle following their liked stars. Around 13 per cent had notion of speaking frankly than before with the families and friends. So this is the change in behaviour taking place. So those who said of influence of being in satellite channels also said that behaviour became active and smart (around 20%). And 12 per cent said had impact on dresses and fashions. About 12 per cent said they are encouraged to be established in life because of satellite televisions. So these are some of the areas that we find both watching channels of foreign language that were done before than the internet use study. So what I wanted to show is how our youth are behaving and their perception and attitudes in their livelihood, in their becoming of next citizenry. So, how they want to be and how they want to like and use their technology.

5

Ancient Communication Policy of Bharatavarsha

Nirmal Mani Adhikary

What I am going to talk on is ancient communication policy of Bharatavarsh. I have used Bharatavarsh but not India. In case of India people use these two words interchangeably but from Nepal's point of view we take a politically incorrect signifier because Bharatvarsha is an ancient geocultural location/area which comprised a vast land, including modern day Nepal, India and other countries. And if we go to the ancient text, for example my research has been in *Natyashastra* including others. And that Natyashastra which is older than *Ramayana* and *Mahabharata* and according to that *Natyashastra*, if you see the geopolitical areas that is sovereign nations according to modern standards were Nepal, Andhra, Anga, Avanthi, Vidurashwath, Drawid, Kaali, Kosal, Gandhar, Magadh, Maalva etc. and out of them only Nepal and very few have retained their sovereignty right back from the Vedic period. All others either have been submerged within modern India or they have got other kind of independent nationhood. So first we need to distinguish between that. When we say Bharatavarsha for India we are making a blunder and the communication policy I am talking here is about that ancient Bharatavarsha. When we talk of policy it obviously requires formal, institutional set up that we won't find in that period. Every era has its own dominant mode. If we go to Vedic and Post-Vedic period, *Yajna* would be dominant mode. For present communication is coming to the dominant one. Earlier it was industrial revolution. So we won't find any sort of communication policy if we look the ancient time from today's paradigm. We need to look it from the paradigm of that time. If we see then we can see communication is part and parcel of culture as well as polity. When we say polity then there are norms with regard to individual and societal communication behaviour, communication ethics. And when we say polity then it will have political dimensions as well as strategical dimensions.

If we go for individual and social dimensions then we will find right from *Rig Veda* where the text it envisions an ideal position for communication "........." Let our minds be in harmony, our horse be in harmony, let our thinking be in harmony, our thought process be in harmony so that we can live for a meaningful living of all together. It starts from that. It has *samndasya sookta* of *Atharva Veda* which envisions how to live in a harmonious way "............" Let's move together, let's live together, let's eat together. "......." my heart becomes yours and your heart becomes mine. Which is called *saridretha*. It has been extensively discoursed in Bharatavarsha poetics. I won't tell it Indian. So if we see then we go to *Manusmriti* period. There you will find "satyam bruyath, preeyam bruyath......" means you speak only those things which are good as well as sweet. Not bad wish in sweet but not harsh which is good. So maintain that in private life but in the political and strategic dimension we find instances from Vedic Brahmana Granthas, for instance the case of Sharma and Panishambad. Pani were outsiders, merchants, coming into this part and sharma performs very well to communicate with them. And if we see the rule in that ".........": Present the good things to your state, your people and try to influence them in such a way that they will be persuaded to have good relation with you. We can see communication policy as the integral part of peace making initiative of the state. If we go to *Purana* period we find in *Bhagavatamahapurana*. There are two types of kings Ben and Prithu. And how Ben communicates and how Prithu communicates. Prithu's rule is transparent, Prithu's rule involves participatory communication and right from the *Rig Veda* we have institutions like *Sabha* which can be equated to house of representative of present day and *Samiti*, a kind of senate. Then we have *Parishd* like council of ministers. And according to *Rig Veda* 3386, this three tier mechanism has various opportunities including advising the rulers matters relating to policy including communication. However as I told you earlier, you won't find communication policy as for say in the streak, standardised format we prefer these days. However, it lays foundation for how to behave with the foreigners, how to communicate in the state level, how to communicate in the societal level and how to communicate in the individual level. Even we can see *Devasur Sangram* is the instance of strategic communication. How Narada went to *Asura* king and tried to influence them by showing the strength of the *Devas*. And sometimes to the Devas trying to pinpoint the weakness they have. So then sometimes he is given responsibility formally to negotiate between two parties. If we go to such instances only then we will find and we can take example from *Ramayana* as well when Vibhishana comes to Ram's place and there is huge discussion between Ram, Lakshaman, Hanuman, Jambavan and all others and while they are examining whether to take Vibhishana in their side or not, they extensively discussed whether he has been trying to penetrate to get information from Ram's side or he has deflected. And in that course as well there is communication ethics and so much communication policy we can find there. And then if we go for *Mahabharata*, thereafter the war was declared over. After Yudhishthira gets Ashwamedha yagya done. Then Narada comes and he put so many questions. Prof. B.K. Kutiala has done Research on Narada and with these more than hundred questions, he lays principles for good governance. And we find how a ruler has to communicate with the people. So if we see there were various types of state mechanisms, from republic to absolute monarchy, to constitutional monarchy and all of these institutions they had their own ways of communicating according to inconvenience with the political system. If we go to more ancient time then *Rith* was the principle behind the creation. In case of *Rith* it was institutional rule which need not be codified. In the *Satyayuga* itself, the rule of *Rith* was over and later on they needed *Dharma*. *Dharma* essentially codified and afterwards all the activities, all the *Purusharthas* they get guidance through *Dharma*. And when we have to make any inferences about communication policy then we can referent from the concept of *Dharma* in Vedic and post-Vedic texts. So in sum since there were diversities in terms of political systems, there were diversities in terms of communication systems as well. We can take two examples one is *Sadharanikaran* mode of communication that is based on *Natyashastra* and *Vakyapadiya. Natyashastra* by Bharathamuni and *Vakypadiya* of Bhartrihari. And its philosophical outline is *Vedanta.* And in *Vedanta* what is ultimate? It is *adhvait* (You have to be one with *parabrahma*) *Ahambrahmasmi.*

So *Sarijetha* is poor concept underlying the *Sadharanikaran* mode of communication so differences are not important here. There are diversities, there is hierarchy, there is asymmetry but somehow the society should work through mechanism of *sarijetha.* All should feel they are one. And it seems applicable within the country for all the fellow country people it is applicable. But, if you go for hierarchical or let us just say in case of institutional of transmission model where you have to influence others then you have to go to *Mimamsa* mode of communication. There what is the ultimate mode? There in *sadharanikaran* mode it was *sarijetha.* Here it is *shanthibhavana,* that means persuasion to do work for the intense of the ... So I am summing up even within Bharatavarsha there were various political systems and those political systems needed different strategic and political communication systems and our ancestors had developed that. And these two models just signify them in different ways. And we have more scope of so many other communication models, communication theories. Maybe we can develop our strategy communication policy in more effective ways if we get to understand our ancient policies.

6

Democratic Elections and Mass Communication

Is South Asia Ready to Meet the Emerging Challenges?

Ashoka Dias

In our region periodic election is common thing. India, Pakistan, Bangladesh, Maldives, Afghanistan and recently Bhutan joined the game. And one common feature in this region is periodically held democratic election. It is a valued common feature. During an election mass communication is entrusted with a vital role. That role has not only legal responsibilities it has also social responsibilities. Why? because the process urges accuracy and fair play.

To take an informed decision at election, information is crucial. Now in this day and age people's choice is directly connected to the role of mass communication. Not only that media acts as a watch dog during elections and ensures transference of process. To better understand the media's role during elections let understand the elements of general elections. The election must be universal, equal, fair, there must be a secret ballet. It should be free, transparent and accountable. Now with that background let us look at media's role during elections. Where do media come in? Quality and time formation is necessary to take an informed decision in the process of selecting representatives to govern in a democracy. It may be in local governmental elections, it may be in state election, it may be in parliamentary elections. In Sri Lanka we have another set of elections called referendums, decide on a particular thing.

So any of these elections media's role is pivotal in keeping the electorate informed. Now election campaigning versus mass media how does this work? In this day and age the diversion of time from political participation is very important. Political participation is a key thing. What is happening today is the political participation is minimising into watching TV or listening to radio. The engagement is becoming more and more media centric and then due to that political marketing, the negative effects are entering into the arena. They go on political marketing and what trust and goodwill and our political campaigns concentrate more on negativity and also what is political campaign negativity? The candidates try to explain the negative aspect of the opponents or the opposite political parties, rather than giving the strength of their party or their own candidate. And on top of that the reportage also is concentrating more on the negative aspect. With all this, the cost of mass communication, the cost for communication expenses during election campaign is going up and up.

The loss by the parties by their own channel to reach masses and the concentration is more on media and media's gatekeepers.

I would like to highlight couple of things with this limited time: during election with the background that I said, Is south Asia ready to meet the emerging challenges? Now during elections we have this system of 48 hours silent period, in certain part of this south Asian region we call it blackout period. For the last 48 hours before the poll campaigning through media is prohibited. Is this practical? When I highlight this, most of the people would think 'this is due to new media phenomena'. No one using the conventional media this result is being challenged again and again.

In Sri Lanka, there are instances like the campaigning ends 48 hours before and the newspapers print. The mode of the newspaper today. It is only the imprint. You change the imprint. For example, if the election is on Friday you have the paper on Friday but the imprint says it is on Wednesday. So how can you catch? Even though conventional media is challenging these things. Then postal body, the elections are structured. They are getting more and more structured to have, to administer elections, the election management bodies need huge man power. So they have government servants working in the election management and the number of postal voters are growing up. In 2005 and 2015 presidential elections, those are the most pivotal elections in Sri Lanka. The margin of victory is less than the number of postal voters. In 2015 presidential election we had a vote base of 15 million voters. And we have 500-1000 postal voters, who are working in election management structure. The silent period is not prescribed during postal vote. It is not in Sri Lanka but most of the other regional countries during the postal voting the campaigns go on. Very targeted, highly concentrated campaigns go on. So are we achieving the desired objective? There was the perception in the colonial ear that the government servants who work in the election management bodies they cannot be fooled. The media can say whatever they want but the government servants will not be changed, they are educated people. That was the assumption. Is it true?

Then these election laws I explained you the cost of election going higher and higher by every election and if someone breaks the law what is the fine? In Sri Lanka most of the election law violation is 100rs. So can you catch a person with that? Then the emergence of new media, IVR servicers, digital billboards, audio-visual advertisements in public transports, mass SMSs. There were instances that the election management body tried their luck to stop mass SMSs. The politicians are creative, the campaign managers are creative, and they are finding new ways. Can that be stopped? In this part of the globe structured political debates are missing. In US, UK you have the structured political debates. Whether it is state elections, or local government elections or presidential elections very structured debates happen. But in this part of the world it is not happening. The television channels, media organisations, they are kind to organise debates but most of the time they are not really structured and only one party participate in the discussion. It is not the debates. In USA, the standards and guidelines are sponsoring political candidate debates in conventional state and local elections formulated and published by the debate advisory standard project. It is funded by few charitable trusts and sponsored by the centre for American politics and citizenship at the University of Maryland. Now in Sri Lanka for the last 30 years, the election law provides to have political debates among the key candidates in the state television. But, it has never happened. Is not it time to give this opportunity for the universities to work on this and organise and structure political debates?

7

Communication in and as Education

A Non-Policy Perspective

Chandrabhanu Patnayak

I wanted to say something about education and communication and I am just trying to link a few things here in terms of policy because the whole conference was started on an interesting note where Rohan talked upon absence of real policy and I take off from there. In the absence of real policy either in education or in communication there are what did we do? We kind of talked about policy, government of India has always talked about making of policy about never in the 70 years gotten down to making one. What they did instead, was every 10 years set up a commission both in communication and in education and these commissions were supposed to give reports. So they took 10 years to deliberate and give reports. And then government filed those reports, did not do much about them and then every once in a while they pick and choose and act upon them and even those actions are very frugal and partial. So as a result of this kind of ad-hokness, I want to make a comment on kind of education that I and all of you here have gone through. This little statement is not about today's students, it is about the kind of education we have gone through.

This is been written out of sense of disillusionment and concommitment anguish from countering a bunch of bright eyed students, trying to cope with the system, design to dumb them without they knowing it. These are our students who are exceedingly nice, well intentioned and utterly descent; they are the result of a civilisation that has forgotten nearly about everything about itself and achieved near perfect indifference to its own culture. Students coming out of elite schools aspire to go to good institutions of higher education and so the government creates centre of excellence. It is difficult to gain admission to this school. Students of these institutions have done what has been demanded of them, they are superb test takers. They know exactly what they needed to do to get an A in every class. In other words these students do not allow themselves to become passionate and invested in anyone subject and they build superb resumes. They are respectful and cordial to their elders for this is the traditional teachers do or as they have been told. They were eloquent on the subject of diversity without having the slightest clue what it means and they are expert in the arts of being expert in public. They are the cream of their generation, masters of the universe, a generation in waiting to run India and the world. But ask them about some basic question about civilisation they will be inheriting, be prepared for aborted eyes, somewhat panic looks.

As of 2014, there are 677 universities in the country, now the number has grown to 800. 37,204 colleges and 11,443 standalone institutions in India as per the statistic of HRD Ministry. There is no dearth of institution willing to give a degree for money, education or skills is not the concern. The highway from Delhi to Rurki which I drove for 5-6 years almost every week, is dotted with shells of buildings posing as private university. Actually any national highway, anywhere in the country if you see a class or fancy building, nothing around it. It is most likely to be a private university. A study done by a private body which says that approximately 18.43 per cent of engineering graduates are employable. This means that almost 80 per cent of them are unemployable. We are very happy to state the positive number. We are all very pleased with numbers in the country the IITs and AIMS and IIMs are cited as examples of success not because of great faculties because of the students. One way of looking at this problem is every student graduating from IITs an IIMs get placed in high salary jobs in the corporate world even before they have finished their final examinations. These students are offered enormous salaries which are rarely turned down. If this is the case then who is teaching in this hallowed institutions of excellence? It could be conjectured that those who did not make it in the corporate world is the one who is teaching there? In a long run this has been a disastrous model. A committee under Anil Kakodkar was formed in 2011 to revamp the 30 NITs, the second run of the IITs and not the 37,200 colleges or the 11,304 institutions. The rationale according to the preamble to this Committee says that these 30 NITs can aid in nation building so what will the lakhs of students in thousands colleges, what are they doing? If they are not involved in aiding nation building exercise then we have much bigger problem at hand. Kakodkar's report is a bundle of homilies, moralities and advice of geriatrics. It was submitted in 2014 to the then Education Minister. The report itself was to my understanding, certainly regressive and out of date. The saddest and most ironical part of higher education in India today is that the system is occupied because of reliance of age, hierarchy and seniority. While the world their students live and learn in has changed. The higher education cannot be rescued from the debts of failure by the same people who are responsible in large measure to bring it there. Those who do not have the stake in its future. A retired nuclear scientist more a bureaucrat should not be recommending anything about the future of anything let alone higher education. Bureaucrats should be kept far away when it comes to reinventing.

In trying to fix this problem, the Government of India and UGC in their combined wisdom decided to emulate the American system as if foreign solution would instantly fix all our problems. They introduced the system to publish or perish by introducing something called API scope in attempt to enhance quality of education, faculty was expected to publish certain number of peer reviewed research papers, attend a certain number of international conferences and so on. Immediately after this rule came into force, the number of academical journal grew experientially. Groups of faculty registered new journal, reviewed each other's papers, and published each other's research. The number of conferences conducted in between January and March has grown for the same reason. In a recently published interview Chomsky laments the market driven education system. While many scholars, educationists and politicians have lamented this terrible trend we continued to perpetuate this opportunate trend with the illusory hope that things will somehow turned out to be fine at the end of the day. What we have failed to adequately appreciate is that this ignorance intended consequence of our education system. It is intended a sign of its robust health and success. We have fallen into the bad and unquestioned habit of thinking that our educational system is broken but it is not. It is working on all cylinders. What our educational system aims to produce is cultural amnesia. A wholesale lack of curiosity, history as free agents and educational goals composed of content free processes. And unexamined buzzwords like critical thinking, diversity, ways of knowing social justice and cultural competence. Our student is an achievement to systemic commitment to producing individuals without a past, groom the future of a foreign country. Cultureless encryptions, who can live anywhere and perform any kind of work without inquiring about its purpose or its ends. We manufactured perfected tools for our economic system that prices flexibility. Regardless of the course of study or specialisation, the main object of the modern education is to chip off the rough remnants of any cultural and historical specificity and identity that might still stick to our students in anyway to make them perfect company men and women for a modern quality and economy that deprives deep commitment. A very appropriate conversation between a father and a son is doing a round in social media today. I thought it might worth quoting here. The son says "dad why do I have to go to school?" the dad says "so can modelled into a state approved homogenous drone that cannot think outside of the prescribed consensus. You learn to repeat information instead of how to think for yourself so you don't become threat to the *status quo*. When you graduate you get a job, pay your taxes in order to perpetuate the corporate system of intent servitude for your political overlords."

This has been the kind of system where I grew up and the generation after me grew up. I grew up and got a job in Indira Gandhi National Open University (IGNOU). When IGNOU first started the people who thought this thing up guided that we should have a system which take education to all those people who did not access to education. So they went shopping, and they found the UK Open University was a best model. They picked it up, brought it and stuck it in our country. What we had then was a system which was completely borrowed from another system and the first course that was launched was MBA. It was for those students who did not have access to education. I worked there for several years and we made audio-visual programme. Even then I had a feeling that this was not going to work because of two reasons. One was unlike in Britain India was a multicultural, multi-ethnic and multi-lingual nation. And centralised programming in English and Hindi is get us nowhere. Especially, if it has to reach the people which got left out of the main stream education. But the experiment continues. Distance education we have spent millions of rupees on propping distance education in this country. Distance education has simply mirrored the formal structured university education. According to one of their latest report, IGNOU has two million students who enrolled and 70 per cent of them drop-out before the completion. What we have is giant elephant. Then we decided as a country to continue what we call technology mediated education. Because technology started growing and we had fit education into that rather than other way around. Every time the new technology came in we tried to fit our education system into it. After long time many technologies like television, radio and so and so forth, we have now come to internet and mobile phones. Radio and the television worked partially but not completely. So if I made a film on joint family system in Delhi but shooting around in Delhi, Haryana and Rajasthan and send that film to Kerala or Manipur, they would kill me. But IGNOU continues to do that as part of sociology department. When we came to using conversion technology in education we (my university) do what is known as skill development or skill training. Everybody told us that we should increase our student base by using technology so tried doing that and found that students who are coming from tribal areas, students who are from rural areas they did not have good enough technology, they did not have good enough internet connectivity, that was not very funny thing for us. And it did not really work.

Let me get back to what we did with communication. What we did with communication is kind of mirrors what we did with education, we basically set up commissions, started taking bits and pieces of thing and putting them to work, most often used systems that we borrowed from everywhere else and tried to fit our own systems into it. New media, this is supposed to be a very democratic system. So we decide to go with that. The technology mediated education and today what we are seeing with social media is whenever anything go wrong with it you throw it on public and say let the public decide and if you do not know what is NEWS today, you leave it and say let the public decide what NEWS is and what NEWS is not. Today we do not have a government policy, what we have is a policy driven by public needs and wants at any given point of time, and these are determined by bits and pieces of policy formulations. They are not complete policies. The government puts out this little fillers and public is supposed to respond to it and that somehow policy. The user generated content that we get from social media has been very useful in education. Today most students believe that the greatest teacher is Google. It has not been yet worked out how we can get structured education from this kind of system. There are tools that can be used for education but I am not sure whether they can replace education anywhere.

8
Communication Policy in Pakistan

Mariam Sheikh

To me the communication for development is utterly the need of our society and academic and profession insight on our mutual contextual issues will help generate innovative thinking and way forward for the betterment of the society. As we know the current territories of Afghanistan, Bangladesh, Bhutan, Maldives, Nepal, India, Pakistan and Sri Lanka they constitute a South Asian region. These are all developing countries and they have long tradition of using communication in order to promote their developmental goals. And to me, all of these developmental countries have similar developmental goals. Communication approaches so far which we have seen in South Asian region have been variously used for promoting immunisation, prevention of diarrhoea, dehydration, HIV, AIDS, Female literacy so these are the sectors which are mainly focused for the communication strategy and development including health, education and skill building.

All these communication campaigns have been in the form of mass media campaigns like radio programmes, posters, street plays and localised outreach through communities and NGOs also through the government. If we talk about the conceptual framework of communication for development, it provides the three basic components as we all know: advocacy, social mobilisation and behaviour change. We know that advocacy mainly informs and motivates leadership to create a supportive environment to achieve various programmes, objectives and developmental goals. While social mobilisation engages and supports participation of institution, community networks to raise the demand for sustainable progress.

While the most important aspect of communication strategy and policy building for the development is the behaviour change communication. According to me this is very important aspect which involves persuasive communication using either face to face dialogue with individuals or groups to inform, motivate, problem solved or planned with the object to promote and sustain behaviour change for the promotion of development. So, if I give you the perspective from Pakistan, communication strategy for the development in the country has been developed and executed by both government and non-governmental sectors in various key sectors of development. In the government sector most of the communication campaigns as we observe are based on public awareness, advocacy or to some extent social mobilisation. The key example is polio eradication initiative. That is by far the largest child health intervention led by the government of Pakistan with the support of also national and international partners. What we observe in the communication campaigns led for the polio eradication is that during each campaign the vaccination teams are able to reach more than 95 per cent children below the age of 5 years, seen by the health authority as a programme with the potential to provide support for tremendous improvement in the quality of health service.

These polio teams have social mobilisers and they are equipped with the media products that are meant for awareness for all the routine immunisation, encouraging the routine immunisation. This strategy was revised by the Prime Minister during the focus group meeting and they thought that we should create a new branding for this campaign and the director was issued and insisted on convergence with routine immunisation and polio eradication, social mobilisation in order to educate community for polio vaccination and routine immunisation. Earlier, the communication unit had agreed upon principles to guide all communication work to generate awareness and create demand who are the broader child had education agenda. But the shift from aggressive and have visibility campaign to content integration and long format programming and repositioning the campaign as a Pakistan driven campaign as a brand with the strong local image was in the strategy. In other sectors if you see that with low health utilisation in Pakistan the maternal, new born child health programme was one of the major initiatives. It was in the area Government of Pakistan identified advocacy and demand creation as one of the major components. So the national communication strategy for MNCH that is Maternal and Newborn Child Health. They designed to improve demand but targeting key audiences with unified health messages using the range of specific communication activities. Advocacy and message delivery were the key elements of this strategy as well. If we talk about another area of development which is skill building the National Skill Strategy (NSS), this strategy was developed in 2009. And it was developed with an objective of providing relevant skills for industrial and economic development assuring quality of skill development improve access, equality and employability of young people. For that, a communication strategy was developed which was aimed at creating public awareness about the role and the utility of the reforms in a skill building and encourages participation of private sector in the policy and policy implementation of NSS. The power of two way communication was a key of this communication strategy of NSS and what they did was, they created public awareness about the role and the utility of the reformed skill building and encourages participation of private sectors through external and internal communication.

Based on this, stakeholder need analysis in this strategy the matrix audience segments, the hurdles created by the lack of awareness and misperception and the goals of message strategy to medicate each have been developed. For each code codemark messages were developed, framed to convey through communication campaigns and activities targeted at the respective audience segment. So modern social change developments such as books, TV commercials, music videos, jingles and documentaries and their focus is mainly on the health and education sector so these are the few examples to give an overview of the communication strategy for the development of Pakistan. Overall when we summarise the tricky elements in Pakistan for communication is developed sector wise. Second, the communication strategy and policy making involves partnership with non-governmental sectors, also with the corporate sector. And also the communication strategy in Pakistan mostly focuses on either advocacy, public awareness or to some extent social mobilisation campaigns. While it is true that need to create a communication strategy for individual projects for development are welcome but there is still a need to develop a comprehensive strategy for the overall development of the country. And what we also have seen that while message delivery, message formats these are very much looked after but the techniques that utilises ICT (Information Communication Technology) are somewhat needed. And I want to focus on the subject of strategic communication of behavioural and social change which are mentioned earlier that I came across the working paper prepared by UNICEF. They talked about contemporary development paradigm that calls for co-ordinated and synergised effort of intersectional and intelligence collaboration to include German rights perspective, commitment to reduce global deprivation, millennium development goals and development agenda for the world fit for children. I strongly agree with this kind of approach to work in coordinated manner and to work on broaden or horizon of the very concept of development and understand the dynamics of communication in the modern practices and modern strategy.

In view of media and communication technology rising trends of communication is broader because the issues are transnational. I strongly promote the idea of having coordinated and integrated approach, comprehensive strategy and policy-making for the communication for the developmental causes. And for this South Asian countries on such forums, like SAARC or any combined joint forums, if they begin or initiate some agenda on mutual understanding, will be great. This will be far reaching. The consequences will be very positive in my opinion because our geographical, economic and political dynamics are somewhat similar so we understand and collaborate in the mutual need of building a communication strategy which is a common goal for all these countries. We have seen over all at many communication initiatives in India as well as in Pakistan have succeeded in enhancing public awareness but somewhat have failed in going beyond awareness to stimulate positive changes in attitude and practices towards creating lasting social change so I think we need critical steps in recasting communication to share behaviours and contribute to positive social change which is very important but this should be on the larger scale. It should not be limited to one project or other. I came across a working paper on social change in

South Asia that is strategic communication for social behavioural change should involve a mix of appropriate multiple and synergetic communication approaches that can encourage individual and social change. With this I would end my presentation here and I would hope that this presentation must have enhanced your understanding about what is going on the other side of your border.

9

India and Her South Asian Neighbours

Connectivity, Culture and Commerce

Wan Aida Wan Yahya

What I'm going to share with you is probably very different in the sense that is more of a broader perspective in terms of South East Asia and considering the sole representative of South East Asia. How India actually influences south-eastern region.

My first introduction to India was through Gandhi, through Shahrukh Khan, and all the other Khans, I grew up in that generation. I was very much influenced by *Kuch Kuch Hota Hai*. As I grew older I became more matured when I was watching *Mother India* and *Patherpanchali* and finally came down to serious business in a way that in 2001, one part of my research the South Asian was actually on historical films and the Asian nations. And I read on Indian history from Sumith Sarkar to writers of now a days. But in a way by looking at Indian history and also Malaysian history, can always say that Malaysia replicates, imitates and follows exactly three hundred years of what happens to India. The only difference between the two nations would be probably just the partition because Malaysia did not have to through such experience. So this is how I came to know India.

The research I have done for the past five years is actually very much on our trends, very much trending nations, trending practices of new media actually. My initial last five years were most focused on South East Asian trends, actually the influences of new media, the transition from films to digital media and online content. And also about how online content and new media helps to preserve cautious value history from those different platforms. Yes, last five years have been very much trending. Before it was mostly on Korea and Japan. It brought me back to India somehow.

In a way I don't intend to talk about policies but as I mentioned how policy implemented in India has in way indirectly or directly influence what has happened whether Asian region or in the South East Asian region specifically. I think when the Prime Minister brought back or rebranded the whole look east policy or act east policy it brought a whole different dimensions, renewed a whole set of relationships and brought back the presence of India and Malaysia in South East Asian region. I think Manipal is very much witnessed with all Malacca Manipal Medical College if you have noticed. Whereby, I think it is very much collaboration with Manipal University and Malaysian Government.

Somebody asked how did the Malaysian Government get the building in Manipal? I won't be able to answer the question, others may know better but it shows the extended of how relationships have evolved; trust in a way may have gotten deeper as the years have gone by. And new policies of this age, 2014 onwards, is in the hopes for the betterment of region. Historically, as I mentioned South East Asia specifically Malaysia is very much influenced by what has happened in India. I think the histories between the nations and the regions can be traced back to probably 14th century. With Hinduism and Buddhism arriving at South East Asia was also very much linked to culture and commerce and trade.

Malacca in Asia being the centre for the trading of Fifteenth century, the relationship between the nations was already bonded and influenced at that time. While I was pondering the best way to tackle sharing what I know with you is the fact that as I progress while developing the paper, it was all about the creation of number of C's throughout. I know this whereby Indian relation and Malaysian relation and South East Asia is very much dominated by culture, very much dominated by commerce, also in modern terms very much dominated by commerce and connectivity in which where was the Look East Policy, Act East Policy but also the whole idea of Asian rebalancing through Indian Asian summits and so far.

On the platform of last Indian Asian Summit on 8th of September, 2016, whereby regional policies were renewed, mostly in security, mostly in trade, and hence in communication in terms of media and broadcasting. However, India has also made an effort to make its presence more felt within the Asian region, in terms of how they can support South Asia as a whole.

Here I would like to put forth a question in terms of what might be the expectation of South East Asian region. I believe South East Asia is taking probably what India is going to do next policy. Especially within the last couple of months of political and global change; with the events, with the Trump's presidency, with China relations in very much what happens next in terms of where India stands and how all the changes would influence South East Asian Region.

And so news of events is very much through media and actually digital media whereby news no longer comes from BBC most of the time, but is mostly online portals. Malaysia after 1998, we reduced the number of news we watched on TV. In Malaysia, people access news from websites rather than national news channels. Content development is very much the trend now, in which digital content is the latest trend. And basically there has to be word of quotient because it comes body-less. Any kind of content can be put online with any kind of excess to anyone. So that is the subjectivity there. However, I think one element in the transitions and in the events that have been occurring in last couple of months is also about South East Asia and South Asia itself taking control of chaos. In a way what I mean here would be Trump's immigration was kind of through lot of countries into uncertainty. But, it was the people's reaction but the nations probably trying to get a grip of where they stand in the whole new structure or new approach of global change.

10
A Study on New FDI Policy for Media

Sathwik

New Economic Policy of 1991 is revolutionary decision taken by Indian Government which widened the process of liberalization and globalization. Though many criticisms are imposed on the new policy there are visible developments in the economy. GDP of India has raised from 274.8 billion USD[1] in 1991 to 2,251 billion USD[2] in 2016. Understanding the triggers, changes, strategies and implications are complex. Two major aspects of the new strategy adapted are: (1) Change in the FDI policy, and (2) Change in the economic

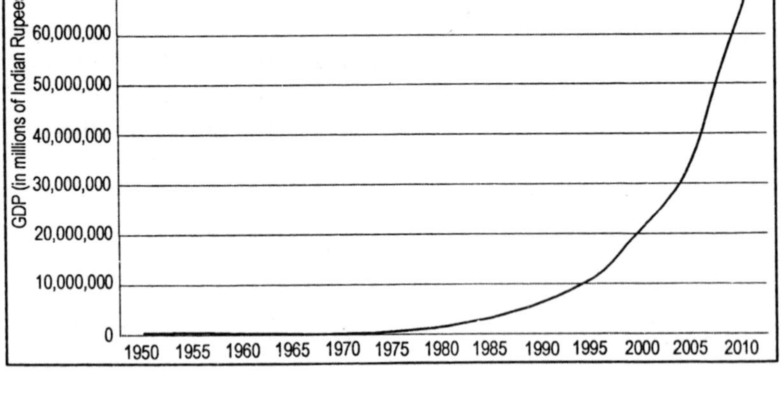

structure. Change in the economic sector refers to the change in the composition of the 3 economic sectors. Service sector which was at 42 per cent of national income during 1991 had increased to 59 per cent in 2013. This shows us the growth in service sector which comprises Media, Transport, Finance, IT, Infrastructure and telecommunication sectors.

After the introduction of FDI, the media industry (print and broadcast) has found exponential growth. Market for print has increased 15 folds that is, from Rs. 10,700 crore to Rs. 153,750 crore during 1991–2008. And Electronic media has expanded its market 30 times (from Rs. 3,900 crore to Rs. 119,500 crore during 1991 to 2008.)[3] By observing this rapid growth after the new economic policy 1991 it is very clear that FDI has affected the market of media. And it is a favourable development for media.

FDI Comparison—India and China

The best way to study Indian economy by comparison with China. As the population is similar and the challenges facing in the economy are similar, it would be very apt to compare Indian economy with Chinese economy.

Table below shows the comparison of FDI flow among India and China.

Year	*India (million US Dollars)*	*China (million US Dollars)*
1980-81	452	1,074
1990-91	1,657	20,691
2000-01	17,517	193,348
2002-03	30,827	228,371
2004-05	38,676	245,467

As shown in the table, FDI flow of India has increased significantly. But when compared to China it is not much satisfactory. China is leading with nearly 6 folds larger. This shows that there are scope for improvement in the field of FDI.

Area astute of FDI Inflows during April 2000 to April 2010.[4]

Sector	*Inflow of FDI (in Rs. crores)*	*Share of the sector*
Service Sector	106992.07	20.35
Computer Software Hardware	44611.13	8.52

(Contd.)

Sector	Inflow of FDI (in Rs. crore)	Share of the sector
Telecommunication	42619.88	7.94
Housing and Real Estates	37614.76	7.13
Construction Activity	36065.91	6.90
Power	21466.46	4.03
Automobile Industry	20863.91	3.90
Metallurgical Industry	13844.71	2.73
Petroleum and Natural Gas	12026.07	2.35
Drugs and Pharmaceuticals	7586.01	1.45
Others	182666.34	34.70
Total	**526357.25**	**100.00**

Progression of FDI approach is additionally in charge of a changing sectoral conveyance of FDI inflows in India. Assembling and different divisions which was overwhelming the total FDI inflows amid 1990 descended because of the rise of service sector as an essential beneficiary of FDI. As seen by the above table service segment has a noteworthy offer in the FDI dissemination.

Following table shows the income in the media.

Year	Print (in crores)	Television (in crores)
1991	10,700	3,900
1992	13,250	4,000
1993	15,550	5,000
1994	22,400	8,500
1995	27,350	13,500
1996	30,500	19,800
1997	31,300	25,800
1998	35,000	33,700
1999	39,200	39,410
2000	43,200	44,400
2001	43,250	45,640
2002	44,240	47,200
2003	46,900	50,900
2004	60,350	58,000
2005	79,300	67,450
2006	97,600	90,250
2007	144,704	104,250
2008	153,750	119,500

As noticed by table above we can notice the growth of market in media sector after the new economic policy. Foreign Trade Development and Regulation Act was passed in 1992. And soon the

FDI started functioning in India. The impact of it can be noticed in the sudden rise of income during 1994. Foreign Investment Promotion Board was established in 1996. And we can see a boom in television media. Conference in Economics and Finance was held in 2006. And various resolutions on liberalizing FDI policies was undertaken. This has made a huge impact on media income as seen in the table.

Modes of FDI impact can be roughly understood as follows:

- Investment on media houses.
- Technological and strategic assistance.
- FDI in other sectors resulting in advertisement.
- Partnerships and tie-ups.
- Production houses in entertainment.
- Introducing global news agencies.

Advantage

FDI has several positive impact for India. Few of them are:

Increase in Capital Inflow

FDI advances more capital inflow into the nation. We have a deficiency of capital in cash as well as material. FDIs will connect this hole by which there will be rapid development of media.

New Technologies

FDI can acquire all the more new advancements in technology which were not received in the nation till now. Better technologies and practices existing in foreign countries can be adapted in India too. Printing technology, broadcasting technology, studio set ups etc. can be improved.

Promotion of Investment

By allowing FDI, we are not only receiving investment from foreign countries, but also as the focus on certain sector increases and the market expands domestic investment will increase. Higher investment will lead to faster infrastructure development.

Increase of Competition

With introduction of FDI competition among media houses increase, this leads to better competency. Competition will lead to increase in quality and efficiency among the media.

Expansion of Market

With FDI import and export gains pace. Indian contents get higher value in foreign markets. Because of competition by achieving better quality attracts more readership/viewership.

Change in Content

The presence of FDIs has certainty changed the way of life and taste example of individuals. Print and Electronic Media try to match the taste of people. And foreign practices, programmes, methods, styles will be adapted in Indian media.

Current FDI Policy in Media Sector[5]

New FDI policy was enforced on April 1, 2011 'Consolidated FDI Policy' according to which following FDI caps are prescribed:

- Terrestrial Broadcasting FM (FM Radio) 20 per cent with government approval.
- Cable Network 49 per cent with government approval.
- Direct-to-Home 49 per cent with government approval.
- Broadcasting Service (broadcasting channels) up to 49 per cent automatic approval, Government route beyond 49 per cent and up to 74 per cent.
- Up-connecting a Non-News and Current Affairs TV Channel (hardware facilities) up to 100 per cent with government endorsement.
- Up-linking a News and Current Affairs TV Channel (hardware facilities) up to 26 per cent with government approval.

- Publication of Newspaper and periodicals up to 26 per cent with government approval.
- Publication of Indian editions of magazines owned by foreign dealing with news and current undertakings up to 26 per cent with government endorsement.
- Publication of Scientific and Technical Magazines/strength diaries/periodicals, subject to consistence with the legitimate system up to 100 per cent with Government endorsement.
- Publication of copy release of outside daily papers 100 per cent with Government endorsement.

Most recent FDI policy amendment is 'Consolidated FDI Policy (Effective from June 07, 2016)'. It suggests following caps for FDI:

- Direct to Home (DTH) up to 49 per cent automatic, 100 per cent Government endorsement.
- Cable Networks has a cap of 49 per cent automatic, 100 per cent Government endorsement.
- Mobile TV up to 49 per cent automatic, 100 per cent Government endorsement.
- Head end-in-the-Sky Broadcasting Service 49 per cent automatic, 100 per cent Government endorsement.
- Terrestrial Broadcasting FM (FM Radio) 49 per cent with Government endorsement.
- Broadcasting Service (broadcasting channels) up to 49 per cent automatic approval, beyond 49 per cent and up to 74 per cent is permitted with government endorsement.
- Up-linking a Non-News and Current Affairs TV Channel (hardware facilities) up to 100 per cent with government approval.
- Up-linking a News and Current Affairs TV Channel (hardware facilities) up to 49 per cent with government approval.
- Publications of Newspaper and periodicals 26 per cent with government approval.
- Publication of Indian editions of magazines owned by foreign management dealing with news and current undertakings up to 26 per cent with government endorsement.

- Publishing/printing of Scientific and Technical Magazines/ journals/periodicals, subject to consistence with the legitimate system up to 100 per cent with Government endorsement.
- Publication of facsimile edition of foreign newspapers 100 per cent with Government approval.

Foreign Investment Promotion Board

Foreign Investment Promotion Board was established in 1996 to promote the FDI flow and to formulate the rules and regulations for investments. All the approvals by Government were conducted by Foreign Investment Promotion Board on behalf of government. FDI in certain areas does not need any special permission. Whereas certain areas need permission from FIPB. But during the Budget 2017-18 presented on 1st February, 2017 abolished FIPB. So far no alternative is done for redirecting permissions. These are two possibilities. Provision of special approval can be abolished, which gives automatic approval for all the sectors. Or there can be another board set up for approval, which is less likely to happen. If all sectors fall under automatic approval list FDI flow is likely to be increased.

Reasons for Slow Inflows

It has been observed that in absolute figures, the FDI inflows in India is impressive but compared to the global flows the share of India is far from satisfactory. Since, India is a late comer in opening up her economy so it is unable to attract sufficient amount of FDI as compared to other developing countries. This is basically linked to its socio-economic set up and policies taken after independence. The review presents broad generalization based on the perceptions of potential foreign investors and independent consultants who interact closely with them. It is argued that FDI is expected to play a supplementary and subsidiary role since it was used as a vehicle for technology transfer. The complete web of regulatory control and bureaucratic intervention accompanied by inadequate infrastructure is also regarded as major constraints. These are some important measurement for checking the low level of FDI inflows in India.

- Legal and Regulatory Framework and FDI Policy.
- Raising FDI Sectoral Caps and other Allied Issues.
- Decentralization of Administration Process.
- Reduce Overly Bureaucratic Facilities.
- Proper Coordination between Centre and States.
- Investment Opportunities in North-Eastern Region.
- Reduce Level of Corruption.

Need for New FDI Policy

Considering the need for increasing FDI flow for media sector and the solution for abolition of FDI Board, there is a strong need to introduce a new FDI policy. Some of the suggestions for it are as follows:

- Formulating Policy for FDI in production houses.
- Removal of government approval provision and keeping only automatic permission provision.
- Increasing FDI cap for news publications to 49 per cent on condition of keeping Indian management.
- Increasing FDI cap for television channels.
- Differentiating News channels from non-news channels.

Footnotes

1. World bank survey.
2. International Monetary Fund: *World Economic Outlook.*
3. Survey by Lodestar Media, Zenith Optimedia.
4. Compiled from SIA Newsletter, Fact Sheet on FDI from August 1991 to April 2010.
5. Consolidated FDI Policy (Effective from June 07, 2016), Consolidated FDI Policy (Effectve from April 1, 2011).

References

Consolidated FDI Policy (Effective from June 07, 2016), Department of Industrial Policy and Promotion, Ministry of Commerce and Industry, Government of India.

Consolidated FDI Policy (Effective From April 1, 2011), Department of Industrial Policy and Promotion, Ministry of Commerce and Industry, Government of India.

Balasubramanyam, V.N. and Sapsford, David, "Does India Need a Lot More FDI?", *Economic and Political Weekly,* Vol. 42, No. 17.

Kohli, Vanita and Khandekar, "The Indian Media Business", Response Books, Delhi, 2010.

Akhtar, Gulshan, "Inflows of FDI in India: Pre and Post-Reform Period", *International Journal of Humanities and Social Science Invention*, Volume 2, Issue 2.

Sen, Chitrakalpa, "FDI in the Service Sector—Propagator of Growth for India?", *Theoretical and Applied Economics*, Volume XVIII (2011), No. 6(559), pp. 141-156.

Webilography

http://dipp.nic.in/English/Policies/Policy.aspx (11th May, 2017).

http://www.mospi.gov.in/sites/default/files/press_release/press_release_7feb08.pdf (11th May, 2017).

http://fipb.gov.in (11th May, 2017).

11

The Role of Communication in Eradicating Polio in India with Special Reference to Public Service Advertisements

Geetha A.J. *and* Vishakha Mandrawadkar

Introduction

Intensive Pulse Polio Immunisation (IPPI) was commenced in India in 1995 when all children under five years of age were given doses of Polio Vaccine on National pulse polio days. The polio eradication effort in India is a joint venture of Ministry of Health and Family Welfare (MOHFW), WHO (NPSP), UNICEF, Rotary International and the U.S. Centres for Disease Control.

Polio eradication campaign is one of the active programmes of Ministry of Health and its partners including UNICEF, WHO and Rotary International since 1995. With the collaborative efforts of various institutions, the number of new cases decreased rapidly over the years. Initially, the Polio programme was threatened by resistance. Minority groups, some communities were swayed by prevailing myths and misconceptions leading them to believe it were part of the Government's strategy to curtail the growth of the population. Fearing impotence, fuelled by insensitive media coverage, there was large scale rejection of the oral vaccine. Recognising that the reasons behind resistance required aggressive persuasion, an intense outreach activity was planned to connect with communities at the ground level. Mass media played an important role in communicating polio eradication programme. Public service advertisements in print media, radio, T.V. has been a regular feature. WHO has officially declared India as a polio free country on March 27, 2014. It was a great achievement in a country like India where people are very hesitant to adopt any new health related projects. Since 1995 various Public Service Advertisements (PSAs) were used in various media.

Public Service Advertisement Media Campaign

The mass media campaign, led by UNICEF, was a collaborative venture which focused on bringing back children to the pulse polio booths. The Government of India managed to reserve its advertisement budget to UNICEF to look after the timely release of advertisements in print media. Rotary International prepared outdoor advertisement including banners and posters, caps and aprons etc. in different languages. The popular advertisement agency Ogilvy and Mather was hired to release social advertising messages in various other media.

Newspaper PSAs

Print advertisements depicting four different appeals were prepared in 13 languages and inserted in all the important publications in India. Advertisements had following messages:

1. Advertisements which informing public of success and challenges of pulse polio vaccine including gratitude for the public's support;
2. Advertisements which explained necessity of repeated doses.
3. Reminder to the guardians of dates of National Immunization Days, highlighting why should they must take their children under five years old to the immunization booth.
4. An advertisement which had appeal from officials of Medical field, requesting parents and persuading them of the advantage of polio drops.

Radio PSAs

Five different radio spots were produced to highlight the various appeals to the parents. They have been broadcasted on 184 AIR stations throughout India. A special radio spot consist of an urge from the Prime Minister of India, was broadcasted in polio ridden districts. A theme song was also aired by 184 AIR radio stations.

TV PSAs

A common theme amongst all the TV PSAs are the children. Children are effective tools to capture and enrapture the audience. Their innocence and shiny smiles are adored by all.

In the first advertisement, the bubbly enthusiasm is captured perfectly as they go door to door, and a child is shown wearing a mask of Amitabh Bachchan and is speaking about being aware. The children are a symbolic representation of our budding future.

The second advertisement is about parents expressing unconditional love towards their children. The simple question raised by Amitabh Bachchan is, "If the parents can provide food, clothing and shelter for their children, why can't they walk two steps forward to protect their children from polio?"

In the third advertisement, a child who has succumbed to polio is shown in crutches, which immediately wins the sympathies of people. As soon as we see his image, our hearts go out to him. The message Amitabh Bachchan tried to portray is the consequences of missed dosage. The more the boy tells his story, more people get moved.

Celebrity Touch

This message was driven home much more effectively by making Mr. Amitabh Bachchan as the central figure in the Public Service Advertisements.

Amitabh Bachchan is a revered actor with a multitude of fans following from all-over the world. He is synonymously known as "The Angry Young Man" after playing many roles of a man against the system, a man who fights against the social injustices and is on the side of the common man. Celebrities in India, share a status almost equivalent to gods. So casting him as the central figure has managed to persuade people as they relate the reel life with real life.

In the initial advertisements, a certain unified optimism was communicated which showed Mr. Bachchan going door-to-door to spread awareness.

Later on, his tone changes to an authoritative note expressing outrage over the insolence and the happy-go-lucky attitude of the masses. Overall, the series of the advertisements have managed to reach the people and establish a bond with them.

Objectives

- To find out the strategies used in PSAs to reach the masses.
- To investigate the role of Public Service Advertisements (PSAs) in Polio eradication in India.
- To find the influence of pulse polio Public service advertisement on the viewers.
- To find out the appearance of celebrity in PSA to fulfil the goal.

Methodology

The study is based on quantitative and qualitative analysis. Both primary and secondary data have been taken into consideration. To find out influence and role of PSAs, a survey method has adopted. Random sampling method parents with the age group of 25-35 is attempted. Around 120 samples are taken with multiple choices based and some of the questions are open ended.

To find out the strategies used in pulse polio PSAs, a systematic review of National advertisement campaigns have been done. Research papers related to Health communication, UNICEF report, Rotary International report, Report of Health Ministry have been reviewed for this purpose.

Analysis and Discussion

Advertisement Viewership Related to Pulse Polio

Fig. 11.1 based on the survey shows that, among 120 respondents, 102 people said that they have come across the advertisement screened in national as well as regional language channels.

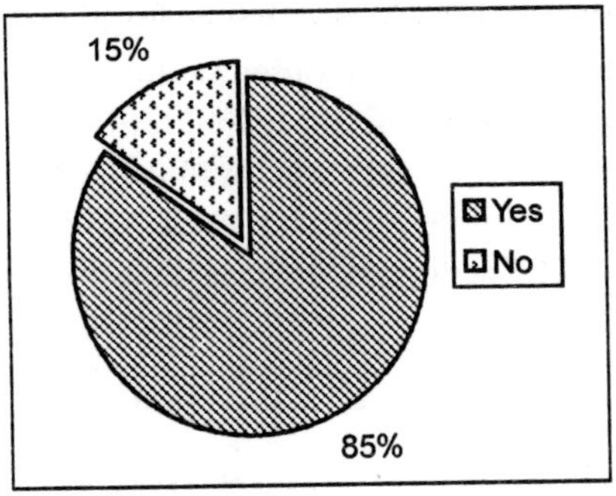

Fig. 11.1: Pulse polio PSA viewership.

Aware of Pulse Polio Advertisement in Television

According to the survey, 81 per cent people mentioned that they are aware of public service advertisement of pulse polio in T.V. Therefore, by this survey, public have come across pulse polio advertisements and it has influenced them. (Fig. 11.2)

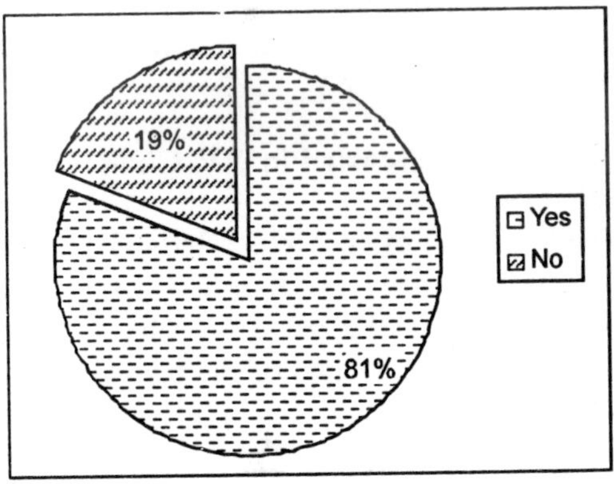

Fig. 11.2: Pulse Polio PSA awareness.

Most Often Exposed Media

Respondent said that television medium delivers more advertisement related to pulse polio compared to other medium. 60.6 per cent people pointed out that television medium delivers more public service announcements and 20 per cent has pointed out outdoor media as second medium which often publicize polio advertisements. And 10 per cent people pointed radio and 4 per cent people pointed out news media. (Fig. 11.3)

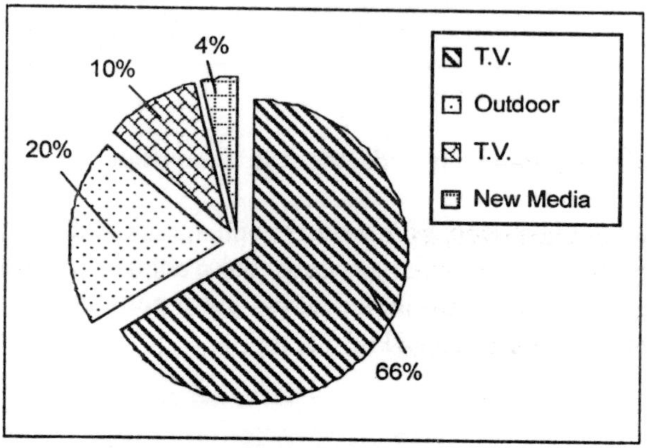

Fig. 11.3: Exposure to pulse polio PSA.

Polio PSA More Often Telecasted in T.V. Channels

Fig. 11.4 shows PSAs more often is telecasted in DD Channels where about 48 per cent have chosen DD out of five channels. According to people's opinion, Zee TV had 5 per cent, Sun networks had 7 per cent, ETv group had 20 per cent and others had 20 per cent PSAs on pulse polio.

Effectiveness of Pulse Polio PSAs

Fig. 11.5 clearly indicates that pulse polio advertisements are followed by the public. Out of 120 respondents, 82 people have agreed they were influenced by pulse polio advertisements.

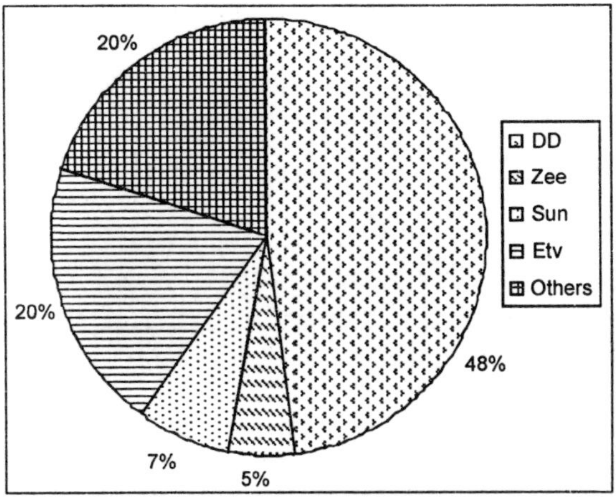

Fig. 11.4: Pulse Polio PSA more often telecasted in Television Channels.

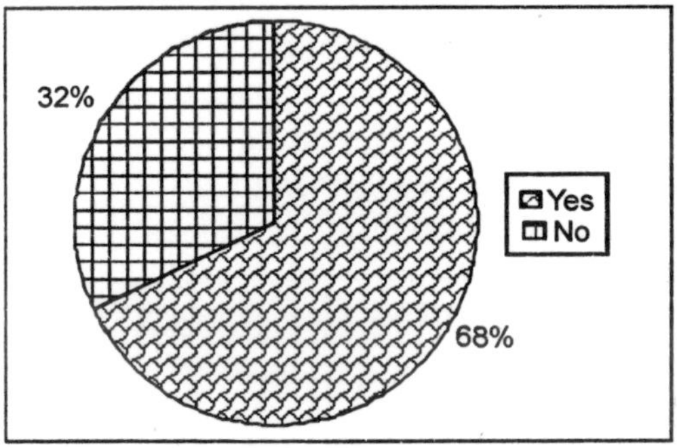

Fig. 11.5: Exposure to pulse polio PSA.

Celebrities Recall

Out of 120 people 61 per cent people recalled Amitabh Bachchan's appearance in P.P. advertisements, 39 per cent people did not recall the brand ambassador of pulse polio campaign (Fig. 11.6).

TV PSA Influence on Public

People have agreed that if there were no social messages appeals in T.V. they would have been forgotten on polio vaccine days. They have also mentioned on the influence of the presence of celebrities in such PSAs.

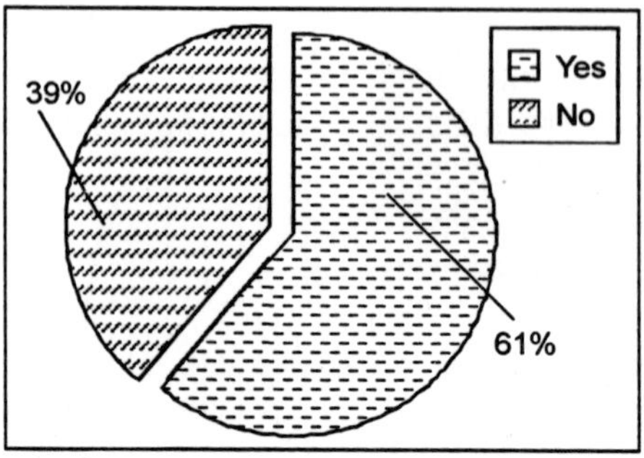

Fig. 11.6: Pulse polio PSA recall.

Drawbacks of Pulse Polio Advertisements

There are some points noted by the respondents about the drawbacks of pulse polio PSAs:

- Dubbing quality was not good. The PSA announcements that are dubbed from national language to regional language was bad.
- Boring.
- Less creativity.
- Lengthy messages.

Qualitative Analysis

Celebrities have played a highly valuable role in announcing campaigns and convincing the parents across the country to vaccinate their children. Bollywood megastar Amitabh Bachchan became the UNICEF Ambassador for Polio in 2002 and began to feature in television and radio advertisements broadcast across India ahead of polio immunization rounds. He and other celebrities such as Shahrukh Khan and Amir Khan made famous the campaign tagline '*Do boond, zindagi keh*' or 'two drops of life'.

The celebrity touch with Mr. Amitabh Bachchan was successful in establishing him as the authoritative ambassador of the polio eradication campaign. The celebrity appeared in four TV spots and four radio spots, dubbed in 13 languages, with free of cost to UNICEF.

"The Angry Young Man" Amitabh Bachchan, who is known as a man who fights against the social injustices and is on the side of the common man, was a intelligent choice for the theme communication. In this case, it has helped massively in creating an image of a goodwill ambassador.

Theme Communication

***1. Do Boond ki Zindagi*:** Four advertisements were prepared with the tag line 'Do Boond ki Zindagi'. Every advertisement ended with the theme—'Pulse Polio Immunization, two drops for life' along with reminder of vaccination dates. Audio-visual advertisements were telecasted four thousand times to reach over 80 million households on National Network DD, as well as to 40 million homes with cable and satellite channels.

2. Har Bachcha, Har Baar: (Every Child, Every Time): In 2009 Mr. Amithab Bachchan was repositioned as the opinion leader. He was the role model to appeal the masses for immunise their kids at every round of vaccinization. The new theme became 'Har bachcha, Har Baar', or 'Every Child, Every Time'.

To popularise this theme three films were produced including a launch film, highlighting the consequences of not vaccinating the kids and the third one being an advertisement, showcasing a polio victim. These three films were successful in highlighting the effect of missed doses.

Impact

By the end of 2010, there were just 42 cases, with just 2 in the last quarter—the lowest ever.

The last case of wild polio virus type 1—the most threatening virus—was reported on 13th January, 2011. India reported its last polio case from district Howrah, WHO on 24th February, 2012 removed India from the list of "endemic countries with active "polio virus transmission". On 27th March, 2014, India has been certified polio free by "The Regional Certification Commission (RCC)".

Conclusion

Though there were many publicity tools employed to eradicate polio in India. Media communication strategy employed by the UNICEF and Health Department played an important role. Because today mass media; especially T.V. media plays a major role in creating awareness. The nationwide public service advertisements broadcasted in T.V. are effective enough to reach people and persuade them to visit polio booths.

References

The Hindu. Plan for polio drops to Haj pilgrims. 2006 November 24. Available from: URL: http://www.thehindu.com/2006/11/24/stories/ 20061124025 41500.htm.

Bonu, S., Rani M., Baker TD. The impact of the national polio immunization campaign on levels and equity in immunization coverage: evidence from rural North India. *Soc. Sci. Med.* 2003; *57*: 1807--1819.

Thacker, N. Polio eradication: window of opportunity. *Indian Pediatr.* 2007; *44*: 81-82.

India Times. Transcript of live chat with Deepak Kapur, Chairman, India National Polio Plus Committee, Rotary International, on November16, 2002. Available from: URL: http:// chat.indiatimes.com

Dyer, O. WHO's attempts to eradicate polio are thwarted in Africa and Asia. *BMJ*, 2005.

'Impact of Celebrity Endorsement on Over all Brand' *http://www.scribd.com/doc/7146790/Impact-of-Celebrity-Endorsements-on-Overall-Brand*

The Financial Express, Brand Wagon, Hotspot, A Brandwagon—Synovate Poll "Celebrities Sell", December 30, 2008.

http://www.iple.in/category/index/polio-immunization-campaigns-1

A Critical Leap to Polio Eradication in India. Working paper 2003, United Nations Children's Fund, Regional Office for South Asia.

Operationan Field Guide on Pulse Polio. Ministry of Health and Family Welfare, India, 2006.

Rural Health Statistics 2014-15. Government of India, Ministry of Health and Family Welfare, Statistics Division.

12

Convergence to Cashless

A Critical Discourse Analysis on Newspaper Content about Cashless Transactions in India

T.R. Ramakrishnan

Globalization and digitization has made the information flow without any limitations in state or national boundaries, which made authors like Thomas Friedman, think that the world is flat. The Earth, a majestic blue marble has about 71 per cent of its surface with water. Today many technologically advanced nations use digitization in conducting business across the globe. Many developing nations take advantage of the cost on mobile and Internet connectivity to network with people across the globe. The operations of many organizations in retail, product development, software development, back office operations have become live with the use of the Internet thereby cutting costs. Companies can close a sale or outsource work to anyone across the world by use of Information and Communication Technology (ICT). The adaptation to ICTs by people has created value for customers of software applications. The speed at which people have adapted to ICTs is the fastest compared to any other mode of communication in the past. The laws relating to the progress of technological advances are unmistakable. Some of the popular laws like the Moore's observation on doubling processor speed every 18 months, Hwang's theory on doubling the memory chip density, Metcalfe's Law on value of telecommunication networks equaling to the square of the number of users have all been commoditized and commercialized for consumer behaviour to change and adapt to screen based communications. Coase's Law specify that as transaction costs decrease, companies complications reduces, and organizations tend to expand until the cost of a marginal transaction internally equals the cost of the same transaction external to the firm. If the cost becomes higher internally in a firm then the option is outsourcing. Deregulation, liberalization and privatization have become popular among many nations across the world. Friedman (2005) cited three convergences that enabled his assumed flat world: (1) new players; (2) a new playing field; and (3) the ability to develop new processes and ways of accomplishing work through horizontal collaboration. New economies as the BRIC are becoming stronger, the concern on the impact of global warming among political leaders, businesses, pressure groups and the public and increasing cultural conflicts in the background of globalization and digitization which are a growing trend. Convergence is at the centre of global change. Convergence of business process evolved in the 1990s followed by convergence of organizations, industries and people create new collaborations, open source participations, new technologies and new products. In a network society scattered people can now share knowledge. Organizations have taken advantage of open-sourcing, outsourcing or global supply chain alliances for development of sustainability and competitive advantage. The evolution of convergence has been a part of human history. Organizational innovation faces different levels of convergence, such as product convergence, functional convergence, organizational convergence, technology convergence, industry convergence and bio-artificial systems (Lee and David L. Olson, 2010). The convergence of EU is an historical unity of economies. Similarly, there are other collaborative convergence such as OPEC, ASEAN, NAFTA, WTO, G5, G7, G8, G20, OECR, Free Trade Agreements (FTA), COP and so on. Hence, convergence has been for stronger networking and gaining value from ICT based transactions. India has significantly contributed to the global economy from the Information Technology Sector. With a strong computer science educational system, many Indian software companies have obtained level 5 certification from the Carnegie Mellon Institute to obtain credentials to verify their software engineering expertise.

Metcalf's Law states that value explodes with membership in a network which leads to the law of increasing returns than economies of scale. Consumers earlier sought for improvements in quality for slight increase in price but the microprocessor industry changed this price equation demanding firms to have higher quality for lesser price (Christensen, 1997). India is an example in increasing membership in the network as almost well connected by mobile phone network and there is an increase in the cellular and broadband subscriptions.

The news industry has transformed with the introduction of cable networks. The Internet technology gave new opportunities for accessing news which has given way for the web sites as an alternative news medium. Today almost all the print and broadcast media have an online web site ID for alternative news access. Associated Press Broadcast Technology has new applications for disseminating news globally. The editorial work of news mediums converges to distribute outputs for television, radio, print and the web thereby changing the reporting assignments. News content is pooled into a common database repository accessible through a common communications protocol in order to achieve consistency. The support from the telecom industry convergence uses both wired, wireless and satellite technology to have information flow flawlessly at good speed with appropriate protocols. Digital convergence has enabled consumers to access any digital content using networking gadgets at any time and at any place (Oshri, 2006).

Digital convergence is the unification of functions, combining technological development with business opportunity. Information Technology (IT) investment has positive impact on productivity acceleration (Corrado, 2007). And a branch of IT is providing rapid growth such as wireless applications technology (WAP), Bluetooth (wireless communication standard), 3G, 4G, 5G mobile systems for better broadband access over wireless. There is also growth in mobility, mass scale and digital convergence (Lyytinen, 2002). These facts have led to push the idea of cashless transactions in the business to consumer commerce in India since November 2016.

Theoretical Background

Communication theories validate that mass media can create significant economic impact. Literature indicates that media theories such as agenda setting, priming, framing, and cultural theory support this concept. The agenda-setting function of the mass media has the capability of raising the importance, through repeated news coverage, of raising the importance of an issue in the public's mind (Severin *et al.*, 2001). The mass media gains attention to critical issues in a country and continuously report on relevant objects suggesting the perception of the public about what they should think about, know about, and have feelings about the issues (Lank, 1959). There are various reports by the media on economic policy that has had an impact in the nation which could influence consumer confidence resulting in their spending habits (McCombs and Shaw, 1972), public policy mood (Durr, 1993) and trust in government (Chanley, Rudolph, and Rahn 2000). The media agenda setting theory, therefore, could have an effect on economic development.

Nation's Economy and Mass Media

Mass media is recommended to be a medium toward impacts on nation's economy. The public can perceive a negative or a positive opinion on the information disseminated by various mediums of mass communication. Social media applications are popularly used and create waves in the mainstream media upon postings from celebrities in politics, sports and entertainment. When the media hyped the housing market correction and subprime mortgage crisis in USA, there was a global economic imbalance. Events such as the Arab spring, the North East community's exodus in India, changeable climate, spread of viral fever, demonetization of currency in India and the elections, had negative multimedia content that caused economies to swing.

The content of mass communication creates fluctuations in the economy as people take cautious decisions which delays business transactions. McGuire (1989) projects media effects of advertising on purchasing; political campaigns on voting; public service announcement on personal behaviour and social improvement; media ritual on social control; emotional behaviour; media images on the social construction of reality; media bias on stereotyping and how media forms affect cognitive activity and style. A more in-depth analysis will be explored on specific media effects in this body of work.

Cashless Transactions

Das and Rakhi (2010) recommended in their study that cash as a mode of payment is an expensive proposition for the Government. But the study showed that above 65 per cent of trades who have a turnover of less that Rs. 1 crore prefer cash transaction over cashless due to the surcharge by plastic card service providers. Cashless (electronic) payment system could reduce currency management cost, follow business transactions, attract more people in the tax net, increase financial inclusion and integrate the parallel economy with mainstream. It can also track the spending behaviour of persons in varied areas which could help the Government to bring more people into the financial inclusion net. This will help to keep a check on unaccounted money or black money in the nation.

The popular types of cashless modes that were available in November 2016 were Cheque, Demand Draft, National Electronic Funds Transfer (NEFT), Real-Time Gross Settlement (RTGS), Immediate Payment Service (IMPS) and Credit or Debit Card. NEFT happens during the working hours of the bank. There are 12 settlements during weekdays between 8 a.m. and 7 p.m. and 6 settlements on Saturdays between 8 a.m. and 1 p.m. There is no maximum limit for NEFT money transfer. RTGS is for high value transactions in real time and gross basis. The transfer happens within 30 minutes of initiation. The settlements happen continually between 8 a.m. to 8 p.m. on weekdays and 8 a.m. to 3.30 p.m. on Saturdays. IMPS is an interbank instant electronic fund transfer service through mobile phones. The same service is used over Automated Teller Machines (ATMs) and Internet banking services. Dave (2016, November 23).

In November 2016, the Reserve Bank of India clarified that prepaid payment instruments can be issued in the form of smart cards, magnetic stripe cards, Net accounts, Net Wallets, Mobile accounts, Mobile Wallets or Paper vouchers. These are classified into 3 types: (a) Closed: issued by an entity where payments can be made only to them, e.g. Ola money and cash withdrawal is not possible, (b) Semi-closed: these are used to buy goods and services with merchants that have a specific contract with the issuer and cash withdrawal is not allowed, e.g. Paytm, SBI Bank Buddy, and (c) Open: these are used to buy goods and services including fund transfer at merchant locations and allow cash withdrawal at ATMs, e.g. Master and Visa cards. Recently, India became popular to the concepts of using e-wallets where the buyer and seller need a smart phone to transfer data, e.g. PayPal. Mobile wallets do not require smart phones or internet connection. You can load money in your mobile wallet *via* IMPS and use it for any transaction ranging from Re. 1, e.g. Paytm (Parekh, 2016). In summary Cashlessindia lists the following tools to be used for business transactions. Banking cards (secure PIN and OTP. RuPay, Visa, MasterCard), Unstructured Supplementary Service Data (USSD)—*99# for interbank account fund transfer, Aadhaar Enabled Payment System (AEPS), Unified Payment Interface (UPI)—converge multiple accounts into one apps, mobile wallets—**Paytm, Freecharge, Mobikwik, Oxigen, mRuppee, Airtel Money, Jio Money, SBI Buddy, itz Cash, Citrus Pay, Vodafone M-Pesa, Axis Bank Lime, ICICI Pockets, SpeedPay** etc. Banks pre-paid cards, Point of Sale, Internet banking (NEFT, RTGS, ECS, IMPS), mobile banking and micro ATMs (Cashlessindia, 2017).

Problem Statement

The public in India suffered since November 2016 by being: anxious, not knowing what to do, curious, scared, unemployed, unable to make payments to liabilities, non-receipt of money for farm produces sold by farmers due to the demonetization of the 500 rupee and 1000 rupee notes worth about 15.44 trillion by the Government of India in order to destroy illegal money. This was a shock to the people in the cash based economy of India and the nation faced a historical challenge to cope up with the daily lives due to the mistrust of the 2 popular currency notes being banned overnight without any prior notice. The endless wait at banks for exchanging notes, people becoming tired and leading to ailments to fatal end of lives were reported especially the senior citizens and home making women. At this phenomenal period of nation's patience with irritancies is remarkable to cope up with daily life. The Government of India at this period, advised over the mass media to the public to use cashless mode of transactions which was new to the majority of the population. Hence to change consumer behaviour to accept cashless method of business transactions was a problem.

This chapter posts a research question: Should the media be a catalyst to political or pressure group's agenda that disrupts the economy? The solution to this question was sought after by applying critical discourse analysis on the grand digital divide, the cash based economy and the political agenda of digital transactions in India.

Review of Literature

There are many articles published from November 2016 till date with respect to the effects of demonetization in India—both in India and abroad. There are about 4 types of transactions in a cash economy, namely accounted, unaccounted, informal and illegal. The Government feared on the illegal transactions that could lead to a loss of revenue collections to the Government as well as escalating crime and terrorism in the country. Hence, the demonetization of the high value currency of Rs. 500 and Rs. 1,000 was sought by the Bharatiya Janata Party (BJP) led by the Honourable Prime Minister Naredra Modi convincing the RBI to execute call back of these two currencies in circulation and abolish the same in India from November 8th, 2016 and the nation is given time till March 2017 through RBI for exchange. This led to the need for consumer behaviour to change to alternative modes of making payments for goods and services (Tax Research Team, 2016).

There are literature that indicate the issues that are faced in a country during the transition period. Some of them are Lack of proper Infrastructure to meet the demand for cash transactions at banks or bank's ATMs. The consumer may not be in a position to adapt to new methods of payments or receipt of cash using electronic methods due to reasons as surcharges, bad networks, complicated, lack of proper smart phone, distrust, time consuming among other issues. Further, the nation need to learn English or Hindi which is a limitation for the majority in India, hence accessibility in language is a limitation. Attributes such as flexibility, mobility and efficiency could solve every day problems of users (Rao & Troshani, 2007). The consumer expectations such on performance, convenience, pricing and quality of goods and services urge towards a feeling of a want or demand linked to social or individual influence will push a person to purchase (Solomon, 2002). The degree of one's involvement in the decision-making process is based on perceived usefulness and risk on that particular goods or service (Blackwell *et al.*, 2008).

The use of alternative methods of payment like using debit or credit makes consumers to spend more (Prelec, 2001). It also leads to an increase in debt as people may have tendency to buy non-essentials which is offered over Equated Monthly Installments (EMIs) (Lee, 2007). The stakeholders to the mammoth of business opportunities in electronic payments include banks, business establishments, electronic transaction processing companies, telecom providers, retailers, consumers and support service providers (Arahao *et al.*, 2016). Transformation and convergence are two forces shaping the evolution of the electronic payments business globally. They will drive some to success and push others to costly failure in the redesigned landscape of 2020 (BNY Mellon, 2014). Most of these studies have used qualitative and quantitative content analysis beyond surveys for consumer behaviour. Trends of technology and social media companies such as Amazon, Google, Microsoft, Airtel and Facebook are seeking entry into payments market. Bit coins without Government control are also in the offing beyond the Government controlled applications. This would lead to be a threat to the banking institutions to those not adapting with consumer expectations.

Thus, we notice in order for the users of cashless transactions, convergence of the services and products of the stakeholders are of prime need. The awareness level of policies with respect to privacy and security amongst the consumers of e-payments has to increase.

Objective of the Study

The objective of the study is to investigate the power of news content and advertisements to influence use of digital medium for cashless transactions.

Methodology

Qualitative research is the analysis that results in the interpretations of depiction of meanings in the researcher's own words (Adler & Clark, 2011). This study engages qualitative research design to evaluate how textual and visual representation persuades using online method of making business transaction in the English dailies in India.

Following a content analysis, this qualitative approach of research vests its unit of analysis as the English daily newspapers of the Bengaluru edition about the news and advertisements on use of digital media for cashless transactions. Berelson (1952) opinion "Content analysis stands or falls by its categories." Content analysis as a research method is a systematic and objective means of describing and quantifying phenomena (Krippendorff, 1980; Downe-Wamboldt, 1992, Sandelowski, 1995). Content analysis is a method that may be used with either qualitative or quantitative data. Discourse analysis is a method of qualitative content analysis.

Critical Discourse Analysis (CDA) is conducted mainly in important social issues and the results are found through discourse analysis. Discourse describes semiotic elements (both text and visuals) of social life. CDA has to focus on the discursive strategies that control the social order and relations of inequality (Fairclough, 1985). CDA engages in multidiscipline nature and examine the relationships between text, talk, visuals, social cognition, power, society and culture. The success is measured by its effectiveness and relevance contributing to change (Fairclough, 1985).

CDA looks into misuse of power by those who hold power like breaches of laws and equality and justice by those who hold power. To these groups the term dominance is reflected. Dominance may be restricted to specific domains and consciously exercised like the case for male dominance over women, white over black, rich over poor etc. If the minds of the dominated can be influenced powerfully for them to accept dominance, and they act out of their own free will based on the interest of the powerful, then hegemony is a relevant term (Gramsci, 1971; Hall *et al.*, 1977). Discourse concentrates on constructing consensus, acceptance and fairness of dominance (Herman and Chomsky, 1988). The credibility of the positive or negative statements that relate to the dominated or dominant groups need to be credible. Hence, persuasive moves such as argumentation, linguistic figures, lexical style, story-telling, structural emphasis of their negative actions and citing credible witnesses, sources or experts given in news reports need to be examined (Van Dijk, 1993). The variation in text can be identified by text analysis on relationship between discourse and genre (Chouliaraki & Fairclough, 1999) and relevant features of genre include the linguistic form and argumentative form of the text (Fairclough, 2003).

This study focuses on fundamental understanding of social problems such as dominance, inequality and the agenda setting of going cashless in business transactions. Based on the secondary data, the study analyzes the complex relationships between dominance and discourse.

Sampling Method

A simple random method was used to select the sample size from the population of the English news daily since November 2016 to January 2017. The effect of the news headers and the visuals upon the content has been framed by critically analyzing the news reports and the visuals of the advertisements about use of digital media for business transactions that has created an impact on the economy. This leads to the discussions on the developments and unease of the digital divide and considers the policy regarding privacy and security on digital media convergence.

Sample Size

Scholars have suggested different sample size for qualitative analysis. Select scholars have set fifteen as the smallest acceptable sample (Guest *et al.* 2006). Charmaz (2006) suggest that 25 are adequate for smaller projects and Ritchie *et al.* (2003) mention it should be less than 50. These figures could be for interviews conducted or documents observed or analysed. This study has considered about 60 as the sample size comprising news reports and advertisements.

Tables 12.1, 12.2, and 12.3 show the dates selected by using the Microsoft Excel function = RANDBETWEEN (8,30) for November; (1,31) for December and (1,31) for January. The random numbers were regenerated multiple times (by pressing F9 key) till there were no clashes between the dates across the four dailies: *The New Indian Express, The Times of India, Economic Times* and *BusinessLine.*

Table 12.1: The random dates selected for accessing news in November 2017

Newspaper	*Dates in November*				
The New Indian Express	15	30	19	27	13
The Times of India	14	22	11	25	10
Economic Times	12	15	22	16	9
BusinessLine	29	25	18	26	17

Table 12.2: The random dates selected for accessing news in December 2017

Newspaper	*Dates in December*				
The New Indian Express	9	10	4	3	21
The Times of India	16	19	2	5	7
Economic Times	20	11	31	17	18
BusinessLine	26	6	8	1	19

Table 12.3: The random dates selected for accessing news in January 2017

Newspaper	*Dates in January*				
The New Indian Express	14	6	2	16	9
The Times of India	22	26	5	12	1
Economic Times	28	30	15	18	11
BusinessLine	29	17	3	10	31

Unit of Analysis

The unit of analysis is the news items or reports and advertisements about using online payment tools during the period of demonetization thereby projecting India to become cashless economy. The study selects the text and images relevant to power and dominance in the dissemination of message in the English newspaper about choosing alternative online mode for receiving and paying money for business transactions.

Data Sourcing Method

This research selected news content and images in advertisements that promote online payment for business transactions during the days of demonetization in India. Data was sourced from the English news dailies of the Bengaluru edition. Some of them were accessed from the online version (HTML/scanned images) of the English daily.

About 50 news reports and advertisements inclusive were sourced from the English dailies, namely *The New Indian Express*, *The Times of India*, *Economic Times* and *BusinessLine*. Categorization was made by identifying cashless, online payment or digital payments. Upon selecting the news item or advertisement, the author had by his own view categorized the content as news that is linked towards cashless transactions.

Categorization of Content

The content is viewed with a framework of qualitative approach to develop the characteristic of interpretation, the categories close to the material. For that scope qualitative content analysis has developed procedures of inductive category development about power and dominance that vests with the influencers of the cashless agenda and the common man's mixed dilemma on confusion, convenience, inconvenience, disruptions, savings and loss.

Coding was carried out in MS Excel for the presence and absence of relevant information to the objectives of the study, thereby quantifying by frequency. Further, the content under each header was reviewed and its relevance was interpreted.

Analysis and Findings

The following documents the results from a content analysis of data sourced from about 20 days at random in the months of November, December 2016 and January 2017 from the archives of the news dailies *The New Indian Express*, *The Times of India*, *Economic Times* and *BusinessLine* totalling to 60 days. The research was designed to analyse the concept of cashless transactions in business due to monetization in India.

On Tuesday 9th November, 2016 at 8 p.m., the nation was taken by surprise by the Television announcement by Prime Minister Narendra Modi stating that Rs. 500 and Rs. 1,000 will cease to be legal tender was not live but was pre-recorded and edited as lack of evidence for being live telecast (Dhar, 2016). The mixed response of the perplexed Indian's showed anger, patience, sacrifice, debates, protests and by enlarge inconvenience caused to the ladies, children and business.

At such a situation prevailing in the nation, there was only one alternative to transfer funds in large amounts and that was by way of cashless transactions which require infrastructure and knowledge to use the software tools that could lead to trust. Only less than 10 per cent of the population can be accounted for using cashless transactions in India due to the core limitations for accessing.

The rules of the market must be addressed prior to the implementation or acceptance of transactions of digital service providers. It is not easy in any country especially in India to accomplish this the next day on the announcement of demonetization in the case of India. It was found in many newspapers that advertisements of category full page or spreads were a common sight by firms such as Paytm, Futurepay, Buddy, Mobikwik, Times card, Freecharge, Snapdeal, Uber, RuPay etc. were prominent in the dailies on 10th November, 2016 onwards persuading people to register for using the apps as an alternative mode for making payments at the time of cash crunch. Such an organized introduction for alternative mode of payments is questionable at short notice. At the speed at which technology and convergence is changing, it is not easy to accomplish a cashless economy briskly. Different forms of correlation, self-regulation, and formal regulation may emerge and conflicts among the interests of companies, customers and citizens are always increasing (Ibanez, 2012). Probably a nation's economy which is stable and as an option of luxury, could exercise but not for those whose infrastructure are bleak and in transition (Lemstra & Melody, 2014). Digitization has helped to have a seamless flow of information in the form of text, voice, data, image and video and technological convergence has been the edge for competitive advantage for infrastructure providers to be market leaders.

Policy-makers are baffled to figure out how to deal with situations of such to create an equilibrium in the economy by inclusiveness irrespective of literacy, income or skill set levels of individuals in society, which is challenging. The outstanding issues on media convergence are Business process re-engineering, training for using nternet or mobile apps and privacy and security in media convergence.

Media convergence has emerged due to the integration of computer hardware, software, telecommunication and networking. At the phase of media convergence, it is rough time for government, companies and individuals to segregate what is "private" and "public" with information flow. The Government would opt for intrusion or surveillance of individual's information for national security. Companies would want hold of individual's information access and details for strategies on competitive advantage. The public would cry stating there is too much of intrusion into their private communication spaces thereby get into a dilemma of what to communicate using which channel to whom.

Hence, a governance system has to formulate a policy to balance between information intrusions into private spaces by commercial or national security interests. Or should the governance be totally against surveillance for commercial interests and be open to surveillance to national interests?, must be debated within public spaces.

The grandest advantage of media convergence is the use of digital media for financial transactions and thereby reduces in carrying cash for expenditure. The Government of India has waived off service tax on car transactions up to Rs. 2,000. The service providers for fund transfers offer various schemes as cash-backs, discounts, reward points and loyalty benefits to stay in use of cards. If majority of the people use digital mode of payment, it would ease scrutiny and can keep track of expenditure. If you forget your pin or lose your card, one can block the card to stay away from frauds. But when hard currency is lost, it cannot be recovered. Going digital also has an advantage of not bothering about getting change. But the problem is hacking, poor network, time taken to do transaction at busy places and fear of losing security information to others.

This study has looked into the news content from different English dailies related to cashless news stories and identified that India is yet not ready by self to exercise cashless transactions for individual spend by the mass both educated and uneducated. Table 12.4 show that 15 days were randomly selected for reading the news from newspapers between November 2016 to January 2017.

Table 12.4: Number of days selected during November 2016 to January 2017

Times of India	*The New Indian Express*	*Economic Times*	*Business Line*
15	15	15	15

The Times of India had more advertisements (see Table 12.5) by software companies that were promoting applications towards digital money transactions over plastic cards and e-wallets. The trend of companies selling digital mobile phones, laptops, online retail (Business to Consumer) and mobile services surged in the advertisements during November 2016 to January 2017. Most advertisements were persuading people to switch to cashless mode of business transactions. An advertisement from RuPay has a slogan—The currency for cash free India. The advertisement states that payments for all shopping and government utilities can be made easily by using RuPay. Another company Paytm mentions "When we change, it is progress. When we all change it is a revolution", "Every indian with or without internet #paytm karo", "Paytm trusted by 160 million Indians." State Bank of India promoted their "Buddy" by stating, "No Cash No Worry Download Buddy—Ask and send money; Recharge and Bill pay, Shop and gift." A software company advertised on their product "Freecharge" by stating, "Cash is not feeling accepted anymore, we are." Ola Cabs Technology Company promoted, "Do not worry. Go note-free with Ola money." However, Uber Software Company allowed cross sales by stating "No Cash No problem Pay with paytm, debit/credit card." Online retailers like Snapdeal campaigned by saying, "No Cash, No worries, Unbox 10 per cent Instant discount on payments made online", "Let life go on cash free", and "Unbox cashfree shopping Snapdeal Unbox Zindagi." Likewise Big Bazaar promoted cross sales on a campaign, "Many more ways to pay for your shopping" use Future pay, Debit cards, gift vouchers, Mobikwik, Paytm, Bajaj Finserv. Freecharge promoted the message "Why worry about 500, 1000 when you can carry 10,000 on your mobile—The fastest way to pay." Times Internet was also in the trail on their campaign, "Black or white Times Card wins over cash", promoting their debit and credit cards. Bank of India tried becoming popular on saying "Go cashless. Go Digital", by using USSD Banking, cards, Internet banking, mobile banking, prepaid cards, easypay, cards at POS. These advertisements were aggressively promoted in print, out of home, online and broadcast media. The advertisements played a major role to provide convenience during the inconvenience faced during demonetization period. There were short supplies of plastic or smart cards, server jams due to overuse and confusions of not knowing how to use these tools for business transactions. Amongst the many players, Paytm became the market leader with maximum exposure both with merchants and consumers. Their market positioning was good and strategies for brand exposure was also excellent by networking with tiny to large businesses in India.

Table 12.5: Number of advertisements selected during November 2016 to January 2017

Topic	*Times of India*	*The New Indian Express*	*Economic Times*	*Business Line*
Mobile Applications	16	1	0	0

The English dailies of Bengaluru edition was searched as per the random dates generated in sampling method. About 10 articles were selected from *The Times of India*, 11 from *The New Indian Express*, 15 from *Economic Times* and *BusinessLine*, totaLling to 51 news reports for analyzing the content. There were 15 articles selected in November 2016, 22 appeared in December 2016 and 14 were selected in January, 2017 (see Table 12.6).

Table 12.6: Number of articles selected during November 2016 to January 2016 about cashless

Month	*Times of India*	*The New Indian Express*	*Economic Times*	*Business Line*
November	4	4	4	3
December	4	5	5	8
January	2	2	6	4

Table 12.7 displays the number of news reports from the select items from Table 12.6 under the frames namely confusions, disruptions, convenience, inconvenience, savings and loss. Not that there are not other frames that reflect to the news stories relating to cashless but these select frames were more prominent in the reports. Majority of the news items, about 29 per cent from the select sample reported on the frame convenience, 20 per cent about savings, 16 per cent on loss, 14 per cent on confusions, 14 per cent on disruptions and 8 per cent on inconvenience. The journalists have never felt like the cash crunch, the alternative digital mode of business transactions

using plastic or e-wallets were inconvenient like the exchange of old to new notes or withdrawals from banks. It is quite obvious with the political agenda to speed up and be at par with other global economies to go digital in one hand and attempts to track funds flow is a gamble with the citizens to change their behaviour overnight.

Table 12.7: Number of article reflecting to select frames during November 2016 to January 2017

Frame	*Times of India*	*The New Indian Express*	*Economic Times*	*Business Line*
Confusions	1	0	2	4
Disruptions	1	2	2	2
Convenience	3	5	4	3
Inconvenience	1	0	3	0
Savings	1	2	2	5
Loss	3	2	2	1

The Times of India contain discourse of wealth and glamour which is evident either by seeing the advertisements in their newspaper or on the news that they promote questioning if paid news was an accepted norm in journalism. A news heading reads 'Paytm's GMV run rate to hit $5bn on note withdrawal', and in the same date 22-11-2016, the advertisements are prominent in the media. On 10-11-2016 a news reads, 'e-wallet transactions surge: cos look to tap merchants', which indicate that e-wallet companies were already prepared with their software tools prior to the announcement of the demonetization. Their marketing strategies were in place especially a company named paytm, when even the banks nor the mobile service providers were on the lead to provide visibility on digital transactions at a short notice.

Bloomberg reported that Central Bank data show that the government-backed Unified Payments Interface logged 3,58,000 transactions in the first nine days of December, shooting past November's 2,87,000 total, as some Indians sought to circumvent the cash shortage that followed the government's surprise graft-busting move on November 8th, 2016. The discourse on cashless or digital transactions, were gaining momentum briskly in India. The UPI system attracted about 2 million registered users as on 12-12-2016 which is just 8 per cent of the target of the 25 million users mentions A. P. Hota, CEO of the National Payments Corp of India and backed by RBI.

BusinessLine spoke to over two dozen players, consumers and merchants to analyse how the payment platforms stack up against each other in terms of cost and efficiency. They found that e-wallets and UPI were briskly getting popular due to their convenient options to receive payments without a burden on capital investments by merchants (Pani, 2016).

Press Trust of India (2016) had a prominent discourse on cashless. Sanjay Pandey, an IPS officer mentioned in a news report that safety of smart card users is important. He narrated that the 40-bit encryption by the Internet Service Providers (ISP) which was mandated in 1999 can be broken by hackers and is a risk for e-business in India. He recommended that getting acceptance of India in the Wassenaar arrangement will enable to access the best of encryption technology or algorithms beyond coming up with a National Encryption Policy.

In order to meet the objective of convenience, with sufficient security for low-value transactions, the Reserve Bank of India relaxed the additional factor authentication (AFA) requirement for transactions up to INR 2,000 across all merchant categories for online 'card not present' (CNP) transactions. This again boosted the digital transactions dramatically. To boost cashless transactions, Prime Minister Narendra Modi had unveiled two schemes—Lucky Grahak Yojana and Digi Dhan Vyapaar Yojana where 15,000 people over a draw system won Rs. 1,000 in their accounts. Cash discount of 10 per cent was provided on the premium amount of general insurance policies and 8 per cent in new life policies for payments made digitally. The Finance Minister too announced tax incentives to small traders accepting payments digitally by reducing deemed profit to 6 per cent for the amount of total turnover or gross receipt received for the Financial Year 2016-17. Companies such as Oxigen Services India, Paytm, Ola Money, FreeCharge, MobiKwik, SBI Buddy, TruePay, JioMoney and Airtel Money have gained a lot of customers, thanks to the government's cashless transactions drive. Of the 26.68 crore PMJDY account-holders, nearly 21 crore (78.71 per cent) had RuPay cards by January 11 (Vinayak A.J., 2017). In the league of the business on cashless transactions, Paytm was highlighted to have got the approval from RBI for payments bank (Pani, 2017).

Hence, it was found from the discourse analysis on "cashless" by interpreting from the readings of select news reports by the sample of this study that the journalist were keen to promote the alternative mode of business transactions than to remain on the cash based economy. There were attempts by the media to educate through news reports on using the applications or mentioning about the pros and cons of going digital.

Conclusion

To conclude on the research, let us go back to the question: Should the media be a catalyst to political or pressure group's agenda that disrupts the economy? It was found that the term "Cashless" was continually used during November 2016 to January 2017 in news headers by journalist. The advertisement also carried the same. The messages in the advertisements and news reports synchronized with the frame convenience at the time of inconvenience caused to the public and the poor during demonetization in 2016. People who had problems with currency had to jump into being a member of the digital era. Millions of new users have adapted to e-wallet more than the plastic card mode of transactions. The incentives related to savings urged people to change and disrupt the business as usual scenario.

It is also evident from this study that different media had different emphasizes to project about cashless with respect to the frames convenience, inconvenience, confusions, disruptions, savings and loss by the news headers and text. There were less images that were seen to these news stories.

In discussing "cashless" in a democratic society, the journalist beyond promoting the political agenda of going cashless and the technology companies who benefit by enlarge, the security and trust was least addressed. It was also evident from the study that people had horror effects on using e-wallets for refunds and the confusions that erupted when oil companies stopped accepting plastic money for a period.

Indeed what links majority of the articles is a sense of modernization to be inclusive in the information society. However, in the framing of the media policy we notice due convergence by the interconnectedness of hardware, software, networking and telecommunications, the issues that India faces are on privacy of individuals digital data open to commercial organizations and the

National security departments for achieving good governance and thereby building trust towards the use of Information and Communication Technology (ICT) tools. Media convergence has emitted persuasion of selecting alternative methods of business transactions in the demonetization scenario in India. It is recommended for an International meet amongst stakeholders with respect to payment systems in a move towards cashless economy in India.

References

Adler, E. and Clark, R. (2011). *An invitation to social research.* Belmont, CA: Wadsworth.

Arahao Ricardo de Sena, Stella Naomi Moriguchi, Darly Fernando Andrade (2016). *Intention of adoption of mobile payment: an analysis in the light of the Unified Theory of Acceptance and Use of Technology (UTAUT)*. RAI Revista de Administração e Inovação. Volume 13, Issue 3, pp. 221–230.

Berelson, B. (1952). *Content analysis in communication research.* New York: The Free Press.

Blackwell, R.D., P.W. Miniard, J.F. Engel (2008). *Comportamento do Consumidor. Tradução de Eduardo Teixeira Ayrosa* (9th ed.), São Paulo: Cengage Learning.

BNY Mellon (2014). *Global Payments 2020: Transformation and Convergence.* New York: BNY Mellon.

Cashlessindia (2017). *Digital Payment Methods.* Retrieved from http://cashlessindia.gov.in/digital_payment_methods.html

Chanley, Virginina A., Thomas J. Rudolph, and Wendy M. Rahn. (2000). "The Origins and Consequences of Public Trust in Governemnt." *Public Opinoin Quarterly, 64*(3): 239-56.

Charmaz, Kathy (2006). *Constructing grounded theory: A practical guide through qualitative analysis.* Thousand Oaks, CA: Sage.

Chouliaraki, L. and Fairclough, N. (1999). *Discourse in Late Modernity: Re-Thinking Critical Discourse Analysis.* Edinburgh: Edinburgh University Press.

Christensen C.M. (1997). *The innovator's dilemma: When new technologies cause great firms to fail.* Cambridge, MA: Harvard Business School Press.

Corrado, C.P.; Lengermann, E.J. Bartelsman; and J.J. Beaulieu (2007). "Sectoral productivity in the United States: Recent Developments and role of IT." *German Economic Review* 8, No. 2, pp. 188-210.

Das Ashish and Rakhi Agarwal (2010). *Cashless payment system in India—A Roadmap. Mumbai: Indian Institute of Technology.* Retrieved from http://www.math.iitb.ac.in/~ashish/workshop/PaymentCardAugust31.pdf

Dave, Riju and Hiral Thanawala (2016, November 23). 3 types of cashless transactions options via prepaid payment instrument for you. Retrieved from http://economictimes.indiatimes.com/wealth/spend/a-look-at-various-cashless-options/articleshow/55508641.cms

Dhar, Sujoy (2016, 27th November). Is Prime Minister Narendra Modi's Note Ban announcement on November 8 was a Pre-Recorded One? Retrieved from www.indialivetoday.com/prime-minister-narendra-modis-note-ban-announcement-november-8-pre-recorded-one/66547.html

Downe-Wamboldt, B. (1992). "Content analysis: method, applications and issues." *Health Care for Women International*, *13*, 313–321.

Durr, Robert H. (1993). "What Moves Policy Sentiment?", *American Political Science Review*, *87*(1):158-70.

Fairclough (N.). (2003). *Analyzing Discourse and Text: Textual Analysis for Social Research*. London: Routledge.

Fairclough, N. (1989). *Language and Power*. London: Longman.

Friedman, T.L. (2005). *The World is Flat: A brief History of the Twenty First Century*. New York: Farrar, Strauss and Giroux.

Gramsci, A. (1971). *Selections from the Prison Notebooks*. New York: International Publishers.

Guest, Greg; Bunce, Arwen and Johnson, Laura (2006). "How many interviews are enough? An experiment with data saturation and variability". *Field Methods*, *18*(1), 59-82.

Hall, S., Lumley, B. and McLennan, G. (1977). "Gramsci on Ideology, in Centre for Contemporary Cultural Studies" (ed.) *Politics and Ideology*: Gramsci, pp. 45-76. London: Hutchinson.

Herman, E.S. and Chomsky, N. (1958). *Manufacturing Consent—The Political Economy of the Mass Media*. New York: Pantheon Books.

Ibanez Colomo, P. (2012). *European communications law and technological convergence*. A.H. Alphen and Den Rijn, The Netherlands: Kluwer Law International.

Krippendorff, K. (1980). *Content Analysis: An Introduction to its Methodology*. Newbury Park: Sage Publications.

Lank, K. and G.E. Lang (1959). "The Mass media and Voting". In E. Burdick and A.J. Brodbeck, eds. *American Voting Behaviour*, pp. 217-235. Glencoe, III: Free Press.

Lee, Sang M. and David L. Olson (2010). *Convergenomics—Strategic innovation in the convergence era*. London: Gower Publishing Limited.

Lee, Jinkook, Fahzy Abdul-Rahman, and Hyungsoo Kim (2007). "Debit card usage: an examination of its impact on household debt." *Financial Services Review,* 16.1, p. 73.

Lemstra, W. and Melody, W.H. (Eds.). (2014). *The dynamics of broadband markets in Europe: Realizing the 2020 digital agenda*. Cambridge, U.K.: Cambridge University Press

Lyytinen, K. and Y. Yoo (2002). "Research commentary: The next wave of nomadic computing." *Information systems research*, 13, No. 4, pp. 377-88.

McCombs, M.E. and D.L. Shaw. (1972). "The Agenda-setting Function of Mass Meida". *Public Opinion Quarterly, 36*:176-187.

McGuire, W.J. (1989). "Theoretical Foundations of Campaigns." In R.E. Rice and C.K. Atkin, (eds). *Public Communication Campaigns.* (2nd ed.) pp. 43-65. Newbury Park. California: Sage.

Orshi, I. and C. Weeber (2006). "Cooperation and competition standards-setting activities in the digitization era: The case of wireless information devices." *Technology Analysis and Strategic Management 18*, No. 2, pp. 265-83.

Pani, Priyanka P.L. (2016, November 25). *As businesses go cashless, digital players vie for market pie*. Retrieved from http://www.thehindubusinessline.com/economy/digital-payment/article9387023.ece

Pani, Priyanka (2017, January 3). *Paytm gets RBI approval for payments bank.* Bengaluru: Business Lin.

Parekh, Raviraj (2016). *10 best cashless payment methods*. Retrieved from http://moneyexcel.com/15775/10-best-cashless-payment-methods

Prelec, Drazen, and Duncan Simester (2001). "Always leave home without it: A further investigation of the credit-card effect on willingness to pay." *Marketing Letters*, 12.1, pp. 5-12.

PTI (2016, December 9). *Encryption Policy must before going cashless*. Retrieved from http://economictimes.indiatimes.com/industry/tech/internet/encryption-policy-must-before-going-cashless/articleshow/55894698.cms

Rao and Troshani (2007, August). "Conceptual framework and propositions for the acceptance of mobile services." *Journal of Theoretical and Applied Electronic Commerce Research*, 2.

Ritchie, Jane; Lewis, Jane and Elam, Gillian (2003). "Designing and selecting samples." In Jane Ritchie and Jane Lewis (Eds.), *Qualitative Research Practice: A Guide for Social Science Students and Researchers* (pp. 77-108), Thousand Oaks, CA: Sage.

Sandelowski, M. (1995). "Qualitative analysis: what it is and how to begin?" *Research in Nursing and Health, 18*, 371–375.

Severn, Wener, and Tankard, James (2001). *Communication Theories: Origins, Methods, and Uses in the Mass Media*. 5th ed.: Longman.

Solomon, M.R. (2002). *O comportamento do consumidor: comprando, possuindo e sendo* (5th ed.). Porto Alegre: Bookman.

Tax Research Team (2016). *Demonetisation: Impact on the Economy*. New Delhi: National Institute of Public Finance and Policy. Retrieved from http://www.nipfp.org.in/media/medialibrary/2016/11/WP_2016_182.pdf

Van Dijk, T.A. (1993). *Elite Discourse and Racism*. Newbury Park, CA: Sage.

Vinayak, A.J. (2017, January 17). *Issue of RuPay cards jumps post-demonetisation*. Retrieved from http://www.thehindubusinessline.com/money-and-banking/ issue-of-rupay-cards-jumps- demonetisation/article9485571.ece

13

Effective Usage of Social Networking Sites in Extension Activities

A Case Study of 'Agriculturist' Facebook Group

Srinivasa Pejathaya and Sushmitha

Introduction

Social media has become a powerful tool that connects millions of people globally from the comfort of our homes; social media is revolutionizing the way business is carried out bringing new ways of communication and exchange of information across the globe. With the introduction of smartphone, social media has become an easily available form of communication.

Built as a tool for socialising Facebook was never purposefully intended to become a revolutionary form of information sharing platform. Tech savvy generation of today found exemplary ways to make use of the technology.

Agriculture in India was in a dire need for a platform where all the problems and solutions be brought under the same roof. Facebook happened to be what the doctor ordered.

Social media plays a major role in enhancing the knowledge and skills of the farmers globally. Through this platform the farmers all around the world can be interconnected where they can gain and share the information and knowledge. Due to which they can improve their agricultural techniques.

There was never a technology such large and cheap that people can be connected globally. Providing direct access between business entities and consumers, Facebook became a bridge between genuine thoughts, relevant information and supply to demand preferences.

Making the idea of global village a reality, tapping into the human need of forming groups, sharing information, providing entertainment and communication social media has achieved so much in such a short span of time.

Extension Activities

In order to remain competitive in a changing world farmers constantly manage and adapt their farm businesses. Making required adjustments in the agricultural practices and updating them from time to time is a really important task. Every new innovation should meet the demand of the consumer.

Agriculture being the backbone of India in the past and in the present it is fitting that the latest technology has found its way. Technology helps farmers access reliable, timely and relevant information.

Complex decision undertaken by farmers requires the collection of a range of information from a number of sources that individual farmer have their favoured information sources which they can access depending on the specific information being sought.

Digital Age

Most people use the internet for personal communication through e-mail, e-commerce and access to information. With the advent of Internet and worldwide web, access to information is unlimited. After initial scepticism some leaders of media industries proclaimed the internet to be the universal information highway and were bullish on its development.

They even found this platform more advantageous where a businessman can effortlessly advertise his products and service without spending on printing and broadcast productions. Moreover, he can be in direct contact with the consumer himself without the interference of the middlemen. Instant feedbacks of the consumers are the addon quality to improvise the business.

Agricultural Extension and Social Media in India

Social media is increasingly being used as a medium of sharing information and creating awareness. Platforms such as Facebook, Twitter, YouTube and blogs have been used to engage with various audiences. The users generate and shape the content. Social media strengths are complementing traditional media in facilitating the shaping of content.

Users of social media have access to platforms like Livestock information, agriculturist, Farmsurge and such others. Farmers and those interested in farming obtain information from these social media platforms. These platforms educate and inform on agricultural matters as well as facilitate the buying and selling of agricultural produce and related products.

The users exchange information and discuss issues concerning agriculture based on experience and knowledge. They also buy and sell agricultural produce and inputs and use pictures, links and videos to facilitate this. This sharing of information facilitates the marketing of the farmers produce and formation of networks. The social media platforms are also used to share links, news articles, information, feedback and for queries.

Agricultural institutions in India have also incorporated social media in their information system. For instance, Vivasayam Karkkalam page managed by Madhu Balan, Public Extension Officer. However not all institutions have fully embraced Web 2.0 as a tool for disseminating information.

Impact of Media Convergence

It is also evident that there is convergence of traditional media and social media to provide and shape content. Agricultural programmes are using social media to engage audiences and obtain feedback. For example, in Kenya, programmes like Shamba Shape Up on Citizen Television and the pull out seeds of gold, in the Saturday Nation have social media platforms. Mkulima Young a radio programme on Coro Fm also obtains its feedback on the Mkulima Young social media platforms.

Literature Reviews

As majority of the blogs were not media related, they could not reach the targeted audiences. Agriculture media utilised the situation and thus started to work on web 2.0 technologies to reach the audience (Rhoades and Aue, 2010).

The Agrarian society is quickly embracing the social media and getting connected with the like-minded agriculturist. Even the villagers have begun to use the social media to come out of isolation which arises due to the nature of their work (Cline, 2011).

Social media overcomes geographical boundaries and creates communities who share common interests. The users also seek out information from traditional social media platforms. Scholars noted that there was a large presence of blogs covering topics on agriculture (Rhoades and Hall, 2007).

Social media bypasses traditional media specifically radio medium which is considered to be one of the very effective mediums of agricultural communication because of its reach and local dialect (Lievrouw and Livingstone, 2006).

Twitter is a best platform to share not only news but also for views, opinion, guidance and advice which has huge need in development support communication (Cline, 2011).

Problem Statement

In the digital era, understanding proper usage of social media platform extension activities is very essential and to do so, there should be a proper model in this segment where people democratically manage a page which serves specific demography of the nation. There is a lack of academic process of research in this area.

Objectives

This study has been conducted with a core objective of understanding the decentralised virtual community in a specified demographic region which resulted in providing benefit to the participant members. Understanding decentralised virtual extension model. Analysing the specific social media platform with various aspects. Critical review of virtual extension platforms.

Methodology

With specific objectives this study uses qualitative content analysis and in-depth interview methodology. Available secondary data is scrutinised based on peer review of various literatures related to the topic. Interview of the admin has been conducted to understand working process of the extension platform and how such social media groups can be viable model both economically and in practice.

Facebook

Facebook is considered to be one of the very effective social media platforms in every field of interest in concern. Credit goes to Facebook for right implementation of web 2.0 technology and virtually community platforms to bring like-minded people together worldwide.

Facebook has over 1.86 billion active users in a month and it increases 17 per cent over a year. As of December 2016, there were 1.15 billion Mobile users who use Facebook on daily basis. And its growth rate is 23 per cent over a year.

Facebook Usage in Agriculture Extension

Facebook Group/Pages	*Details*	*Target users*	*Region*	*Followers/ Members**
Mkulima Young (Young Farmer) (https://www.facebook.com/mkulima.young)	This is an information sharing platform, widely used by young farmers. This page is started by Joseph Macharia, emerging farmer of Kenya. This page shares agri related advices and market information.	Young farmers	Kenya	**1,03,673**

(Contd.)

Facebook Group/Pages	*Details*	*Target users*	*Region*	*Followers/ Members**
Livestock Information and Marketing Centre (https://www.facebook.com/groups/Livestock.TN/	Members of Livestock Information and Marketing Centre share information related to livestock production, management, marketing and such related issues.	Agricultural stakeholders related to livestock	Tamil Nadu, India	**96,755**
Agriculturist (https://www.facebook.com/groups/Agriculturist/)	Members from farming sectors of Dakshina Kannada and rest of Karnataka share agriculture related information, graphics, videos and other details for sharing, knowledge, advice as well as for business purpose.	Agricultural stakehol-ders	Puttur, Karnataka	**44,343**
Natural farming Development Centre (https://www.facebook.com/groups/NaturalFarmingTN/).	Members share information about organic farming, permaculture, hydroponics, aquaponics, Natural Repellents and related to natural farming techniques.	Farmers interested in organic and zero budget agriculture	Tamil Nadu, India	**18,976**
Turmeric Farmers' Association of India (https://www.facebook.com/turmeric.farmers)	Turmeric farmers started this page to stabilize price of turmeric in the market. Here turmeric farmers community connected through this page and share crop and market details, which results in stable price for turmeric in the Indian market.	Turmeric farmers	India	**5,291**

(*Contd.*)

Facebook Group/Pages	*Details*	*Target users*	*Region*	*Followers/ Members**
The Weekend Agriculturist (https://www.facebook.com/groups/theweekendagriculturist/)	Here members can volunteer themselves as free labour for agriculture on weekends. Even they can contribute essential materials to needy farmers.	Farm volunteers	India	**14,900**
National Ecological Producers Association (APNE) (https://www.facebook.com/anpe.peru)	Ecological farming information is shared in this page.	Farmers	Peru	**6,060**
Vivasayam Karkkalam (Let us Learn Agriculture) (https://www.facebook.com/groups/madhualan)	This group dedicated to share details about latest and successful agri techniques and technologies. There will be continuous debates and discussions about usage of technologies, and which will result in improved versions of tools. This group started and monitored by Mr. Madhu Balan, Public Extension Officer.	Farmers and others those who are interested in agriculture	Tamil Nadu, India	**16,043**

*as of 15 March, 2017.

Analysis of Agriculturist, Facebook Group

The Facebook group, AGRICULTURIST (www.facebook.com/groups/agriculturist) plunged on 27 October, 2007 by tiller Mr. Mahesh Puchchapady. Mr. Mahesh Puchchapady and Ramesh Delampady being group admins manage to monitor the policies related to adding members to the group along with keeping a tab on ethical and legal aspects of the contents discussed in the group. An active

Facebook bracket holds 44,343 members, on 15 March, 2017 count. More than 35 per cent of members are active in posting, sharing and discussions and an average of 13 discussions will be posted everyday and each discussion gets 150 to 200 likes speaks its endorsement. Attractive 590 albums, 4000 photo captions and 800 videos posted by the members made its canopy to cover quite a large extent. It is highly notable that, the contents posted are related to agricultural and allied services explains its focused interest. While taking into account of videos, more than 85 per cent of videos fetching the demonstration of agricultural related facilities and equipment. The ideal duration of 150 seconds made easy glue to video as observed by multimedia experts.

The objective of the group is to cater the needs of tech savvy agricultural community who belongs various strata of society. This group provides communication platform where people share their experiences and put the question forward and others try to provide the practical solution. The purpose of this group is to standardise agricultural practice into a professional business entity.

The founder and admin of the group Mr. Mahesh Puchchapady (Agriculturist and Journalist) opines in stressing the proper admin policy channelized them to entertain agricultural related contents and stick to the core purpose of the group. The Facebook platform evolved in many avenues providing more members to come face to face, telephonic and virtual contacts, in return discuss their problems related agrarian sectors. The practical exposure farmers always on toes to discuss, disseminate and proper guidance to needy people.

The group has organised various agriculture related programmes in collaborations with various governmental, non-governmental and private organisations which gave the opportunity to interact each other and understand better on virtual community.

Findings

After analysing available secondary data and statistical figures related to the group, and also understanding the in depth interview of the founder and admin, this study has the possibilities to list out various aspects in correlation with communication strategy with ICT based agricultural extension activities. The findings of the study are very much practical on the basis of theoretical framework.

- Using Facebook platform is a very efficient and economically viable model.
- Cloud based social media networking with demographical categorisation is more applicable than universal or offline or traditional media communication.
- Need based extension activities will always yield the benefit.
- Discussions are monitored by the admin panel to cater the core objective of the group.
- Posting self-made demonstration video is very innovative and practical in nature.
- Comments are based on the post rather than gossips, hence purpose is served.
- Facebook to Face2Face concept is very unique and innovative practice in development communication domain.
- Virtual group organizing venue based events in collaboration is with various bodies is good thing to practice.
- Percentage of active user is lower than essential.

Conclusion

Developing countries like India has done tremendous experiments in the domains of agricultural extension. Social networking media platforms like Facebook has been a better cloud based free platform to create a virtual community and communicate among like-minded people. Demography based virtual groups like Agriculturist made it possible to provide 'Facebook to Face2Face' for elite groups of agricultural sectors and it can be a unique and innovative practice which can be followed by other groups of same or different sectors of the society. India has not achieved agricultural development in a proper and scientific manner, even though experimenting lot of extension activities. In this juncture this study concludes that efficient and constructive usage of such platforms will yield the reap and benefit agri-business sector of any country.

eferences

ıdres, Dustin and Woodard, Josh (2013). *Social media handbook for agricultural development practitioners*. Publication of the FACET project implemented by FHI 360 for USAID. https://communities.usaidallnet.gov/ictforag/node/427.

Babu, S.; Glendenning, C.; Okyere, K. and Govindarajan, S. (2012). *Farmer Information Needs and Search Behaviour. Case Study in Tamil Nadu India*, IFPRI.

Chowdhury, A., and Hambly Odame, H. (2013). "Social Media for Enhancing Innovation in Agri-food and Rural Development: Current Dynamics in Ontario, Canada." In W. Ashton and A.S. Carson [Eds.], *The Journal of Rural and Community Development*, *8*(2), 97-119. Available at: www.jrcd.ca

Chui, M., Manyika, J., Bughin, J., Dobbs, R., Roxburgh, C., Sarrazin, H., Sands, G., and Westergren, M. (2012). *The social economy: Unlocking value and productivity through social technologies.* McKinsey Global Institute. Retrieved from http://www.mckinsey.com/insights/high_tech_telecoms_internet/the_social_economy

CIARD (2012). *Case Study: KAINET.*

Dennis, E. and Merill, J. (2006). *Media Debates Great Issues For the Digital Age.* California: Thomson Wadsworth.

Diekmann, F., C. Loibl and M.T. Batte (2009). "The Economics of Agricultural Information: Factors Affecting Commercial Farmers' Information Strategies in Ohio." *Review of Agricultural Economics*, *31* (4): 853–872.

Diem, K.G., Hino, J., Martin, D. and Meisenbach, T. (2011). "Is extension ready to adopt technology for delivering programmes and reaching new audiences?" *Journal of Extension*, Article number FEA1, *49*(6). www.joe.org/joe/2011december/a1.php

Gakuru, M.; Kristen W. and Stepman, F. (2009). *Inventory of Innovative Farmer Advisory Services Using Information Communication Technologies.* The Forum for Agricultural Research in Africa.

Hall, K., and Rhoades, E. (2009). *Influence of Subjective Norms and Communication Preferences on Grain Farmers' Attitudes toward Organic and Non-Organic Farming.* The Association for Communication Excellence in Agriculture, Natural Resources, and Life and Human Sciences Conference, Iowa City, Iowa.

Kaplan and Haenlein (2009). *Harnessing social media in agriculture. Report for New Zealand Nuffield Scholarship Fund.* http://www.nuffield.org.nz/uploads/media/S_Stanley_2013_Final_Report.pdf

Lievrouw, L.A. and Livingstone, S. (2006). *The Handbook of New Media. Social Shaping and Social Consequences of ICTs.* London: Sage Publications.

Mbugua, D.K. *et al.* (2012). *Information access and rating of delivery pathways by smallholder dairy farmers in central Kenya.* KARI, Naivasha.

Ndung'u, M.N. and Waema, T.M. (2011). *Development Outcomes of Internet and Mobile Phones use in Kenya: the household's perspectives.* Info, 110-124.

Newbury, Elizabeth, Humphreys, Lee, and Fuess, Lucas (2014). "Over the Hurdles: Barriers to Social Media Use in Extension Offices", *Journal of Extension*, Article number 5FEA1, 52(5). www.joe.org/joe/2014october/a1.php

Ruth, A. and Lundy, L. (2004). Reaching Florida urban opinion leaders: Uncovering preferred communication channels. *Journal of Applied Communications, 88*(4), 7-21.

Sulaiman, R.S. and Davis, K. (2012). *The New Extensionist: Roles, strategies and capacities to strengthen extension and advisory services*. Global Forum for Rural Advisory Services, November 2012. www.g-fras.org/en/gfras/157-the-new-extensionist.html. Davis, K. and Heemskerk, W. (2012). *Investment in extension and advisory services as part of agricultural innovation systems*. Module 3 of Agricultural Innovation Systems: An investment sourcebook. Washington, DC: The World Bank. elibrary.worldbank.org/doi/pdf/10.1596/978-0-8213-8684-2

Synovate Ltd. (2009). *A long way down the DIGITAL DIVIDE starts to narrow*.

14

A Study on Kannada Online News

Consumer's Interaction Across Platforms

Deepak B.J. and Padma Rani

Introduction

The rapid development of online interactive communication technology plays an important role in connecting people in the society (Hyunjin Kang, 2013). In traditional media, journalists are the one who produces the news and audience consume it. Since the emergence of new media, the scenario has slightly modified.

Online media are given an opportunity for easy and fast access to news and it lets the user comment, share, posting, and so on (Mitchell & Guskin, 2013) and organizations are able to interact directly with users and monitor trends of news stories. The active participation of users also gives new ideas while responding to valid criticism and complaints at the same time (Rosendale, 2015).

Social networking sites have become an integral part of the modern world today. Social websites are amongst the most visited sites on the internet (Alexa, 2008). The potential of Social Media to engage so many users at a minimal cost makes it as an ideal tool for traditional media organizations to reach out maximum users (Rosendale, 2015).

India is witnessing an increase in the number of middle class that speaks different languages has led media organizations eyeing on localized news in regional languages. Owing to the significant diversity of Indian print media, brands have gradually started integrating a regional component. The print media industry has started utilizing digital medium for a consolidated service offerings and many of the companies have expanded their existing portfolio to include new delivery formats such as social media platforms, mobile news app etc. (FICCI, Indian Media and Entertainment Industry Report, 2016).

Review of Literature

Traditional media organizations have started paying attention for the rapidly changing online technologies. The digital advancement is not only a challenge, but also it is creating an opportunity for marketers, advertisers, and media content creators to establish a healthy relationship with the users. With the tremendous growth of social media and online applications, it is believed that traditional mass media will employ more innovative social media sites to enhance long term user relationships (Guo, M., 2011).

Social media networking sites such as Facebook, MySpace and Twitter offers various features to help the users to socialize on the online platform. Users share messages, music, videos, pictures and most other standard forms of expression. The social media sites are the most viewed and visited sites on the internet (Alexa, 2008). Since last few years, the growth of social media is tremendous offering different focuses, features and designs.

The potential of Social Media to engage so many users at a minimal cost makes it as an ideal tool for traditional media organizations to reach out maximum users (Rosendale, 2015). Many public and private organizations are turning to Social Networking Sites such as Facebook and Twitter, which gives an opportunity for easy and fast access to news and it let the user comment, share, posting, and so on (Mitchell & Guskin, 2013) and organizations are able to interact directly with users and monitor industrial trends. The active participation of users also gives new ideas while responding to valid criticism and complaints at the same time (Rosendale, 2015).

Reuters Institute Digital News Report-2016 pointed out the direct consumption of news has been increased through social media. Facebook maintained its domination when it comes to news consumption and production. Across 44 per cent sample says they use Facebook to access news.

Breaking news, news related videos, live streams and other visual content are being prioritized in social media sites. The website owners have given priority for publishing news in localized/native format. Since the middle of 2015, the news media organizations have started uploading news instantly on Facebook. Social media is just one way of reading online news and the majority of users ends up being a consumer of a news website. Social media sites encourage discussion and sharing the news. The 24 per cent of online news users share news *via* social media sites. The study proved that users are more interested in sharing news, which is related to politics, business, technology, environment, and so on (Reuters Institute Digital News Report, 2016).

Social media allows the organizations to produce a highly sophisticated and persuasive branding message and instantly publish globally. But, Gowdy (2009) believes building the user credibility and efficiency is more important than quick upload.

News we bsite users are more likely to engage in higher quality discussion than Facebook users. Facebook users are more likely to express an 'opinion' on the issues being discussed. These opinions are largely homogeneous. On the hand, website user's comments are ideologically balanced, relevant, solutions to the problems being discussed, extract detailed information from other users and address another participant (Rowe, 2015). It is essential to understand how regional print media utilized popular social media sites and the user's response to it.

Method

Social media networks are the best tool to attract the mass in a minimal time and cost. Regional Medias are adopting technological changes in the field of Journalism and the users started accessing the news through social media (Rosendale, 2015).

According to Indian Media and Entertainment Industry report 2016, Print media industry have started utilising digital medium for a consolidated service offering and many of the companies have expanded their existing portfolio to include new delivery formats such as social media platforms, mobile news app etc. It is evident that Kannada regional print media organizations are also have started adopting social media to reach the target audience in Karnataka.

Udayavani is popular regional print media organization in Dakshina Kannada, Karnataka. The online presence made them more popular. It is essential to understand, how a regional media organization is able to reach more than 1 million of users in 5 years through social media. This chapter attempts to document the user's reaction and interaction on Udyavani news website and its social media sites.

The qualitative content analysis method is employed in this study. The Facebook, Twitter and Youtube pages of Udayavani, Kannada newspaper, Karnataka, is analyzed to understand the user's response and interaction. In this study, a total of 1,521 Facebook posts analyzed from 10th February, 2017 to 10th March, 2017.

Facebook

The posts are mainly divided into two main categories i.e. *Hard News* and *Soft News*. Up-to-the-minute news and events that require immediate reporting are considered hard news. On the other hand, features and news that is considered background information or human-interest are considered as soft news.

This study also adopted three sub-categories i.e. *'Positive Response', 'Negative Response' and 'Neutral Response'* to understand the user's response to the Facebook posts. A user's response which has positive reply such as 'Good', 'Happy', 'Congratulations', 'Love' and so on are placed under 'positive response' category. The user's comments which have negative aspects such as 'bad', 'sad', ' angry', 'hate', 'abusive words' and so on are categorized under 'negative response'. Some of the users take a neutral stand by passing comments such as 'oh', 'ok', 'so?', 'may be', 'opinion on a certain issue which supports both negative and positive indirectly'. These types of comments are placed under the neutral category.

Further, two more sub-categories were adopted to understand the user's response to the brand (Udayavani) i.e. *The positive and negative response*. These two options will help to understand how users convey their gratitude for receiving news. At the same time, how people react to the certain posts which they have disagreements.

Twitter

Twitter is one of the popular Social networking services. It let the users post and interact with messages and tweets. But the Tweets are restricted to 140 characters. The registered users can post the tweets and unregistered can only read them. Udayavani also has a Twitter account. It publishes breaking news in the English Language.

Youtube

Udayavani created its YouTube Channel on 23 August, 2016. It has received 24,634 views and 73 subscribers. Udayavani has not uploaded any videos from February 10th to March 10th, 2017.

Analysis

Udayavani Facebook page has obtained total 11,34,311 *Likes* and 11,15,818 *followers* (till 10th March 2017). It received Minimum 1,400 *Likes* to maximum 1,700 *Likes* everyday. It supports the fact, as Reuters Institute Digital News Report (2016) pointed out: the majority of users consumes news *via* social media. It is true that the traditional media organizations have aggressively integrated several Social Media to connect with their users (Guo, M. 2011).

Udayavani received 37,375 user Likes per month. It has published at least 3 posts per hour. It has uploaded 21-40 hard news and 10-17 soft news everyday. In a month, it published 1,570 posts of which 1028 are hard news and 542 are soft news. It is evident, Udayavani focused more on the Hard news.

Soft News

Udayavani updates soft news between 7 a.m. to 11 a.m. and 8 p.m. to 11 p.m. on Facebook. Surprisingly, it updates the first post exactly at 7 a.m. everyday. It maintained the frequency of half an hour to upload soft news stories. The soft news includes feature stories, stories of temples, astrology, motivational stories and birthday wishes. The user's responses to soft news are poor compared to hard news. But, the user participates actively when it comes to feature stories which have religious touch and birthday posters of the celebrities. The study pointed out that, user's comments are well composed and positive.

Hard News

Udayavani publishes hard news between 11 a.m. to 10 p.m. It uploads news as early as it receives information. Quick update on the news proves the fact that Udayavani gives importance for the immediacy of uploading news. There were few incidents where the Udayavani failed to convey the actual news through the featured images. They published a headline, website link, hashtags, featured image and also try to create the curiosity by using attractive words. The study noticed that the comments are more hidden in the hard news category. And, users have given philosophical advice, opinions, suggestions, provocative and abusive words.

In China, users have given more attention to soft news; followed by finance news, economy news, social and political news (Shen and Liang, 2014). But, when it comes to users of regional media like Udayavani in India, they have preferred to read more hard news than soft news. For instance, majority of the soft news related to lifestyle, friendship, love, the relationship gets less response. Other hand, hard news which comprises Breaking news, sports, crime reports receives highest user participations.

The Designs of Udayavani posts are done professionally. The users can access the Udayavani news website by clicking on the featured image and URL published on the Facebook page. All hard news is published with featured image, link, title/caption, and hashtags. On the other hand, soft news also followed the same pattern except for more than 5 lines of brief information published in the status box.

User's Response

On an average, all the posts have positive and negative user opinions. The coastal Karnataka readers and Kannadiga user's response are high where they could relate themselves. This study noticed that users are passing comments based on the personal experience or its collective intelligence. For instance, if there is news on the reservation for the Social backward community, the beneficiary (user) tends to pass positive comments. On the other hand, non-beneficiary showcases his/her disagreements. This type of user behaviour was noticed throughout the study.

Users did not prefer much to *like, comment* and *share* posts which are related to crime. Especially, news related bloodsheds. It shows that Facebook users are not really interested in reading the news which disturbs their emotions. But, they do show sympathy for violence on women, child, animals, and poor people. This study identified that user's response is high when it comes to crime reports which have national integrity and patriotic feeling. For instance, Indian soldiers killed terrorist/Pakistani soldiers.

Facebook users are interacting more on positive news coverage. It shows majority users would like to share good news stories. They tend to pass more negative comments when the user misunderstood the post or controversial news stories of their favourite personalities.

Users tend to take a neutral stand when they come across stories such as Economic growth or destruction of natural resources (chopping of trees to build a flyover). The users show concern for the destruction of nature, at the same time they would like to have flyover to get rid of a hectic traffic jam. In such kind of dilemma, users tend to pass neutral comments.

Users are responding similarly when a post is universal in nature. For example a success story of a man. The user passes comments in the same passion. On the other hand, some of the users pass irrelevant comments. For instance, a celebrity's birthday post—a user commented saying "RIP". And, some of them write about a job opening in the comment box.

Social media sites encourage discussion and sharing the news (Reuters Institute Digital News Report, 2016). The users themselves start replying to each other's comments and argue with the Facebook comment box.

Live video is the updated features in Facebook. In a month, Udayavani did three live video interactions with the users. On 4th March, Udayavani has done a live video interaction on the topic of 'how to face the exam'. In the history of the Kannada journalism, this was the first of its kind to have live facebook interaction with the parents and students. This video has received 15 thousand views,

956 likes, 73 shares and 238 comments. The majority of the users have appreciated the work of the Udayavani.

Another live video had done on the occasion of world women's day (8th March, 2017). This video has received 18 thousand views, 1.1 thousand likes, 71 shares and 242 comments. The majority of the users have conveyed their best wishes through comments. On 21st February, Udayavani had uploaded a video of a collapsing a Kotelingeshwara Chariot. This video has received 459 shares, 31 comments and 503 likes. It indicated user's response for live videos are more than information through text and featured image.

Throughout a month of observation, only three others had given a positive response to the brand (Udayavani) by commenting *"Thank you Udayavani", "Good story", "Good news"*. On the other hand, users responded aggressively when they come across news stories which disturb their belief. They have passed negative comments such as *"Stop publishing fake news", "stop posting cheap news", "old news", "we will unfollow Udayavani, if you don't delete the post", "publish true stories", "Udayavani is a porn site", " you fools, give scientific details", "why do you waste our time"*. They also used abusive words to express their disagreement and they tend to follow the similar opinion/comments passed by the fellow user.

As Hyunjin Kang (2013) says an online reader who would like to show off her or his knowledge to others by sharing news stories without reading carefully. Some extent Hyunjin's argument is right in the case of Udayavani Facebook users. The study noticed a few users don't read the actual news published on the website. They pass comments just seeing the featured image published on the Facebook page. Some instances where fellow users have suggested other users read the actual news story before passing the wrong comment/opinion.

Facebook recently introduced animated sticker option on Facebook. It will help the users to express their feelings *via* animation/ cartoon. They can use these animated stickers instead of Emojis. The study noticed that the usages of stickers are limited among the Udayavani users. A user has sent 10 different animated stickers on a movie related posts under soft news category. Another instance where different users have sent many animated stickers one by another. As this study said earlier, users tend to pass comment/express the same passion of fellow users. These animated stickers have a comical approach. Due to this, user's comments might not have taken it seriously.

Udayavani's Response to Users

DeAndrea (2012) says website owners can promote positive impressions by strategically responding to or ignoring the content posted by others. The admin's interaction with the users is minimal in Udayavani. But, Udayavani responds to users only if it is required. As DeAndrea said, the Udayavani is strategically ignoring the unnecessary interaction with the users. An interview of senior sub-editor of social media and online department, Udayavani said that Udayavani does respond to direct inbox messages from the users who give valuable tips for improvisation, appreciation, and disagreements. But, it does not respond for funny memes, funny messages, good morning and good night messages of users.

Hidden Comments

It is interesting to know that, many user's comments are being hidden in Udayavani's Facebook Page. The study reveals that the comments are hidden for controversial news stories, corrupt politician, actor, and religious news stories. Senior sub-editor of Udayavani revealed that Udayavani hides the controversial/unrelated comments by the users. It hides the comments to avoid the unnecessary controversy or riot or communal clashes in the society.

Usage of Hashtags

Adopting new technology advancement is helping Udayavani to reach more people everyday. The hashtag helps users to search a specific post in the Facebook search bar. Udayavani utilized the hashtag feature effectively compared to other Kannada news website's Facebook pages such as Kannada Prabha, Coastal Digest, Daijiworld, News Karnataka and so on. The usual hashtags are #Udayavani #Kannada # KannadaNews. There are hashtags also used in Kannada language words such as Kannada, Kannada Sudhi and Udayavani. The Hastags are bilingual in natrue. This feature provides the opportunity for the users to find the all related news in a particular place (Facebook wall). This is one of the reasons users might feel Udayavani is more user friendly.

Twitter

Udayavani started its Twitter account in May 2011. It has 14.5 thousand followers and 3,957 likes. Till date, it has done 14.7 thousand tweets. Udyavani witnessed poor response from the users. The breaking news is being updated on Twitter. But, the interaction of the user is minimal. It does not have a page in Kannada. All the tweets are being published in English. It might be one the major reasons for getting less response from the users.

Findings and Conclusion

Udayavani is the leading Facebook page among other Kannada newspapers. It has received total 11,34,311 *Likes* and 11,15,818 *followers* (till 10th March, 2017). Facebook users 'Likes'. It hints the fact that Udayavani being successful on social media platform. Being timely oriented, providing accurate news and maintaining professionalism is the best way to have a rapport with the users. Udayavani does attempt to meet these parameters. Study noticed that Udayavani quickly adopts new technologies and changing trends in media. It updates news exactly at 7 a.m. and gradually it habituates users to access news regularly.

This study pointed out the interaction of the user is more in the hard news category. But, they have given a higher positive response to the soft news. User preferred to interact/share the more positive news. Users participated actively in community/religion based news stories. The study noticed that the user's comments are being hidden more in controversial news stories. They tend to do personalized interaction and follow the same commenting pattern of fellow users. The Facebook user responds positively if the news post is in favour of them *vice versa*. Udayavani have published many crime reports in which users didn't like to participate in crime news stories. Users have shown sympathy for the violence on innocent. Sometimes, a group of users, argues/discusses on a topic in a comment box. The

Study found that few users pass comments without reading the actual news story. They also liked to share knowledge and give reference links to make their point stronger. Compared to text and featured image posts, users have participated actively in a Live video conversation. Throughout a month of analysis, Brand (Udayavani) has received a less positive response. The interaction of Udayavani with users is minimal. Udayavani responds only when it is necessary. User interaction for English post on Kannada page is less.

This chapter suggests Udayavani concentrate more on positive posts, more community/coastal based news coverage, avoid bloodshed posts, adopt innovative ways to make users to generate content, more live video interactions, develop a strategy to make users read the story completely.

Further research can be done to identify the difference between website users and social media users and also study can be done on how others express their emotions using the updated features such as 'like', ' love', 'laugh', 'wow', 'sad', and 'angry' in Facebook.

Udayavani focused more on the Facebook as a main social media network to grab the attention of the user. The Udayavani does not have Kannada Twitter Account. It uploads the breaking news in the English Language. It might be the one of the main reasons why people are not interacting much with the Udayavani. This study also pointed out that, Udayavani does not have comment option on its website. Udayavani also failed to utilise the YouTube channel to the maximum.

References

Brake, D.R. (2014). *Sharing Our Lives Online: Risks and Exposure in Social Media*. Palgrave Macmillan, 191-193.

Ceron, A. (2015). "Internet, News, and Political Trust: The Difference Between Social Media and Online Media Outlets." *Journal of Computer-Mediated Communication*, 487-503.

DeAndrea, D.C. (2012). "Participatory Social Media and the Evaluation of Online Behaviour. *Human Communication Research*, 510-528.

Guo, M. (2014). "Relationship Marketing in an Online Social Media Context: Newspaper *Versus* Television Brand Websites Comparison." *Journal of Media Business Studies*, 1-26.

Guo, M. a.-O. (2011). "Building Online Relationship: Examining Social Media Utilization on Traditional Media Websites." *International Communication*

Association (pp. 1-31). TBA, Boston: International Communication Association.

Holton, A.E. (2015). "Reciprocity and the News: The Role of Personal and Social Media Reciprocity in News Creation and Consumption." *International Journal of Communication*, 2526–2547.

Hyunjin Kang, J.K. (2013). "Does Online News Reading and Sharing Shape Perceptions of the Internet as a Place for Public Deliberations?" *Mass Communication and Society*, 533–556.

John, N.A. (2013). *Sharing and Web 2.0: The emergence of a keyword.* The Hebrew University, 167-182.

Kammer, A. (2013). "Audience Participation in the Production of Online News Towards Typology." *Nordicom Review*, 113-126.

Mitchell, A., and Guskin, E. (2013). *Twitter news consumers: Young, mobile, and educated.* Washington, DC: Pew Research Center. Retrieved from http://www.journalism.org/2013/11/04/ twitter-newsconsumers-young-mobile-and-educated/

Nic Newman with Richard Fletcher, D.A. (2016). *Reurters Institute Digital news report.* England: University of Oxford.

Rogers, A.S. (2001). *India's Communication Revolution.* New Delhi: Sage Publications Inc.

Rosendale, J.A. (2015). "New Communication Technologies in Organization Communications and Branding: The Integral Role Social Media Now Play." *Florida Communication Journal*, 49-59.

Tang, L. (2013). "Consuming news in Chinese cyberspace: a case study." *Continuum: Journal of Media and Cultural Studies*, 740-751.

Willnat, L.W. (2013). "Online Media and Political Participation: The Case of Malaysia." *Mass Communication and Society*, 557-585.

15
Communication in Healthcare

Moulya Jeevanram *and* Shrigouri S. Joshi

Introduction

Today, much of our communication takes place online and *via* our phones, which means our ability to effectively communicate, without technology sometimes suffers. But in many professional fields, real communication is a necessary skill that can greatly affect others. In fact, communication plays a very important role in the medical field as practically everything that happens in a hospital and other medical environments rely on and involve communication.

Objectives of the Research

- To understand the way of communication in medical field especially in the hospitals.
- To see the importance given to communication in the selected hospitals of Moodubidire.
- To examine the patient's expectation and how good communication helps in curing the diseases.
- To know the doctor and patients' perception with regard to effective communication in the clinics.

Research Methodology

Observation and interview methodologies have been adopted for the present study. We have selected three hospitals out of which one is Government hospital and two are private hospitals. 100 patients are interviewed and 20 doctors are interviewed with fixed questions. The questions were designed to know the answers from the patients on the following:

1. Type of the disease.
2. Duration of the disease.
3. Knowledge about the disease.
4. Knowledge about his doctor and medication.
5. Patient's satisfaction with doctor's way of communication.

The questions asked for doctors are on:

1. Their experiences with the patients.
2. Patient's mentality with regard to the treatments.
3. Use of communication in medication.

The out-patients are interviewed after the appointment with the doctor. And in-patients have been interviewed in the respected wards. Visuals of the interviews have been recorded and analyzed.

Types of Communication in Medical Field

In the medical field, communication can take on different forms, with several being the most commonly used and crucial: written, non-verbal, and verbal communication. Here are some examples of these types of communication and why and how they are such a huge and impactful part of success in the medical field.

1. Written Communication

Written communication is one of the most important means of communication used in the medical field. Hospitals are extremely busy places, so it is not practical to rely on face-to-face communication, which is where writing comes into play. Being able to write succinctly, quickly, and neatly is an integral skill to have in the medical field, and one which you should already start practicing and perfecting in undergrad. Oftentimes, your ability to clearly communicate *via* the written words will be instrumental to a patient's care, and there will be no room for mistakes or illegibility.

Medical records must be detailed and properly written as they help keep track of the care and history of patients; missing information can be dangerous to a patient's health. Using a shorthand can be helpful when updating records, but only if everyone who may read that patient's chart and records understands the shorthand since it is widely used.

Additionally, in most cases, a patient will have a board or sign in their room that will have written on it things like the date, the patient's name, their doctors, the diagnoses of the patient, and other pertinent information that may need to be easily accessed and referenced. Being able to write and update that board in a way others will understand will help medical personnel to better aid the patient.

2. Non-verbal Communication

Besides verbally communicating with a patient and their family, as well as your co-workers, non-verbal communication and cues are important to consider as well.

Patients and co-workers will respond to your energy, attitude, and emotions, so you need to be careful how you portray and project yourself as it will affect the atmosphere of a patient's room and your relationships with your patients and co-workers.

Facial expressions, voice level and tone, eye contact, posture, and more, can all undermine or aid your communication with a patient or peer. For example, answering questions in a monotone voice or with short answers will make it seems like you are uninterested, unengaged, and in a hurry to be somewhere else, which will make a patient feel unimportant. Be careful to take into account how you are non-verbally communicating when you are verbally communicating.

3. Verbal Communication

There are two types of verbal communication that are most important to master: co-worker communication and patient/family communication.

- *Co-worker Communication:* Nurses and doctors and other medical personnel all have to communicate with each other in order to provide the best care possible to their patients. Sometimes that communication is verbal, in which case it is necessary to be as clear and concise as possible and use terms everyone understands since there may not be written instructions accompanying your verbal communication. Possessing exceptional written and verbal communication skills are essential as there is no room for miscommunications or misunderstandings when it comes to a patient's information and care.
- *Patient and Family Communication*: As a doctor, nurse, or other medical professional, you will be communicating with patients frequently and will often be the main point of contact and source of information for both the patients and their families. Because of this responsibility, being able to effectively communicate verbally is a crucial skill to have in the medical field. You will be tasked with answering questions, providing diagnoses, explaining conditions and treatments, and more. Being friendly, informative, and knowledgeable is key to creating a good relationship with your patient and their family and establishing yourself as trustworthy, honest, supportive and empathetic.

Without communication, verbal, non-verbal, written, and otherwise, the medical field would be much less efficient and organized, and patients would suffer for it. In the medical field, communication goes beyond just patient charts, treatment instructions, and medical records; it extends to the way we interact with patients, families and peers. Communication affects the success a person may have in the medical field so having exceptional verbal, non-verbal, and written communication skills will help you go far in the medical field and enable you to better engage with patients and co-workers.

According to information shared in a recent article from Becker's Hospital Review, a popular hospital magazine "...more than a quarter of hospital readmissions could be avoided with better communication among healthcare teams and between providers and patients." Communication in a healthcare setting is one of the most important tools hospitals have for providing great patient care and improving patient satisfaction. However, lines of communication can frequently be crossed and lead to lower patient satisfaction scores, illnesses or worse. Every patient who comes to a hospital has a team of people involved in providing care throughout their healing process: from doctors and nurses to housekeeping and culinary teams, and even their family and loved ones. With so many parties involved, it is understandable that mis-steps in communication could occur. The US Department of Health and Human Resources says: "We take communication and patient care seriously and train our team members to break down these communication barriers to provide excellent patient care."

HHS Chief Operating Officer, Bobby Floyd, noted: "Patients have a higher expectation of the type of care they are going to receive when they are in the hospital, and not just from nurses and doctors but also from support services such as housekeeping. They expect courtesy and communication from all whom they interact with, including room technicians and other frontline team members.

"As such, the caliber of frontline team members has changed: they need to not only perform their day-to-day duties, but also be able to address needs of patients. They are expected to speak with the patient, determine his or her needs, and solve problems, all in a proactive manner", says HHS article in the magazine.

Observations

The hospitals which we have taken for the study, it is found that they have immensely used displays on the walls. Especially in the government hospitals the information on the diseases such as Malaria, Dengue, Cholera, Filarial, Typhoid, Tetanus, Tuberculosis and other contagious diseases have been displayed and also the information about vaccinations, available government services, health schemes also have been displayed on the walls. And the 20 doctors whom we interviewed have expressed that it is 90 per cent communication works on the patient. If the communication is done properly diseases can be easily cured, they said. This is a common feedback we got in the doctor's interview.

Discussion

Basic communication skills in isolation are insufficient to create and sustain a successful therapeutic doctor-patient relationship, which consists of shared perceptions and feelings regarding the nature of the problem, goals of treatment, and psychosocial support. Interpersonal skills build on this basic communication skill. Appropriate communication integrates both patient- and doctor-centred approaches.

The ultimate objective of any doctor-patient communication is to improve the patient's health and medical care. Studies on doctor-patient communication have demonstrated patient discontent even when many doctors considered the communication adequate or even excellent. Doctors tend to overestimate their abilities in communication. Tongue *et al.* reported that 75 per cent of the orthopaedic surgeons surveyed believed that they communicated satisfactorily with their patients, but only 21 per cent of the patients reported satisfactory communication with their doctors. Patient surveys have consistently shown that they want better communication with their doctors.

The principles of patient-centred medicine date back to the ancient Greek school of Cos. However, patient-centred medicine has not always been common practice. For example, in the 1950s to 1970s, most doctors considered it inhumane and detrimental to patients to disclose bad news because of the bleak treatment prospect for cancers. The medical model has more recently evolved from paternalism to individualism. Information exchange is the dominant communication model, and the health consumer movement has led to the current model of shared decision making and patient-centred communication.

Benefits of Effective Communication

Effective doctor-patient communication is a central clinical function, and the resultant communication is the heart and art of medicine and a central component in the delivery of health care. The three main goals of current doctor-patient communication are creating a good interpersonal relationship, facilitating exchange of information, and including patients in decision making. Effective doctor-patient communication is determined by the doctors' "bedside manner," which patients judge as a major indicator of their doctors' general competence.

Good doctor-patient communication has the potential to help regulate patients' emotions, facilitate comprehension of medical information, and allow for better identification of patients' needs, perceptions, and expectations. Patients reporting good communication with their doctor are more likely to be satisfied with their care, and especially to share pertinent information for accurate diagnosis of their problems, follow advice, and adhere to the prescribed treatment. Patients' agreement with the doctor about the nature of the treatment and need for follow-up is strongly associated with their recovery.

Studies have shown correlations between a sense of control and the ability to tolerate pain, recovery from illness, decreased tumour growth, and daily functioning. Enhanced psychological adjustments and better mental health have also been reported. Some studies have observed a decrease in length of hospital stay and therefore the cost of individual medical visits and fewer referrals.

A more patient-centred encounter results in better patient as well as doctor satisfaction. Satisfied patients are less likely to lodge formal complaints or initiate malpractice complaints. Satisfied patients are advantageous for doctors in terms of greater job satisfaction, less work-related stress, and reduced burnout.

Observations

Out 100 patients whom we interviewed randomly are of minor injuries, headache, gastritis. They are all well aware of their disease and medication. Here also we found that the common expectation of a patient is good communicative doctor. For many a patient's good doctor is the one who asks about his details and speaks well.

Few Problems Observed

There are many barriers to good communication in the doctor-patient relationship, including patients' anxiety and fear, doctors' burden of work, time limitation, fear of litigation, fear of physical or verbal abuse, and unrealistic patient expectations.

Deterioration of Doctors' Communication Skills

It has been observed that communication skills tend to decline as medical students progress through their medical education, and over time doctors in training tend to lose their focus on holistic patient care. Furthermore, the emotional and physical brutality of medical training, particularly during internship and residency, suppresses empathy, substitute's techniques and procedures for talk, and may even result in derision of patients.

Non-disclosure of Information

The doctor-patient interaction is a complex process, and serious miscommunication is a potential pitfall, especially in terms of patients' understanding of their prognosis, purpose of care, expectations, and involvement in treatment. These important factors may affect the choices patients make regarding their treatment and end-of-life care, which can have a significant influence on the disease. Good communication skills practiced by doctors allowed patients to perceive themselves as a full participant during discussions relating to their health.

Doctors' Avoidance Behaviour

There are reported observations of doctors avoiding discussion of the emotional and social impact of patients' problems because it distressed them when they could not handle these issues or they did not have the time to do so adequately. This situation negatively affected doctors emotionally and tended to increase patients' distress. This avoidance behaviour may result in patients being unwilling to disclose problems, which could delay and adversely impact their recovery.

Discouragement of Collaboration

Physicians have been found to discourage patients from voicing their concerns and expectations as well as requests for more information. This negative influence of the doctors' behaviour and the resultant nature of the doctor-patient communication deterred patients from asserting their need for information and explanations. Patients can feel disempowered and may be unable to achieve their health goals. Lack of sufficient explanation results in poor patient understanding, and a lack of consensus between doctor and patient may lead to therapeutic failure.

Resistance by Patients

Today, patients have recognized that they are not passive recipients and are able to resist the power and expert authority that society grants doctors. They can implicitly and explicitly resist the monologue of information transfer from doctors by actively reconstructing expert information to assert their own perspectives, integrate with their knowledge of their own bodies and experiences, as well as the social realities of their lives.

Suggestions

- Better to include a training or course for medical students on communication.
- Doctors must not be trained only about the test and medication. They should be taught basic sense of behaviour.
- Internees must understand the local people's pulse (not technically speaking).
- Especially in the government hospitals the way of diagnosis must be improved. Rather than making it a public show, they can keep it in systematic private rooms as in the private hospitals.
- As per the observation time constraint is the major problem in the detailed tests. So the concerned hospitals and the doctors must see through the availability of timing.

Limitations

- Lack of responses because of fear and anxiety from the patient's side.
- It was not found proper to disturb the hospital atmosphere. So questionnaire method couldn't be done.

- Lack of time.
- Off season for the diseases.

Conclusion

"The patient will never care how much you know, until they know how much you care." (Terry Canale in his American Academy of Orthopaedic Surgeons Vice Presidential Address)

Doctor-patient communication is a major component of the process of health care. Doctors are in a unique position of respect and power. Effective doctor-patient communication can be a source of motivation, incentive, reassurance, and support. A good doctor-patient relationship can increase job satisfaction and reinforce patients' self-confidence, motivation, and positive view of their health status, which may influence their health outcomes.

Most complaints about doctors are related to issues of communication, not clinical competency. Patients want doctors who can skilfully diagnose and treat their sicknesses as well as communicate with them effectively.

Doctors with better communication and interpersonal skills are able to detect problems earlier, can prevent medical crises and expensive intervention, and provide better support to their patients. This may lead to higher-quality outcomes and better satisfaction, lower costs of care, greater patient understanding of health issues, and better adherence to the treatment process. There is currently a greater expectation of collaborative decision making, with physicians and patients participating as partners to achieve the agreed upon goals and the attainment of quality of life.

References

Asnani, M.R. (2009). "Patient-physician communication." *West Indian Med J*, *58*(4):357-61.

Clark, P.A. (2003). "Medical practices' sensitivity to patients' needs: Opportunities and practices for improvement." *Journal of Ambulatory Care Management*, *26*(2), 110-123.

Duffy, F.D., Gordon, G. H., Whelan, G., Cole-Kelly, K., and Frankel, R. (2004). Assessing competence in communication and interpersonal skills: The Kalamazoo II report; *Academic Medicine*, *79*, 495-507.

Heisler, M., Bouknight, R.R., Hayward, R.A., Smith, D.M., and Kerr, E.A. (2002). "The relative importance of physician communication, participatory decision-making, and patient understanding in diabetes self-management." *Journal of General Internal Medicine, 17*, 243-252.

Renzi, C., Abeni, D., Picardi, A., Agostini, E., Melchi, C.F., Pasquini, P., Prudu, P., and Braga, M. (2001). "Factors associated with patient satisfaction with care among dermatological outpatients." *British Journal of Dermatology, 145*, 617-623.

Safran, D.G., Taira, D., Rogers, W.H., Kosinski, M., Ware, J.E., and Tarlov, A.R. (1998). "Linking primary care performance to outcomes of care; Journal of Family Practice", *47*(3), 213-220.

Sullivan, L.M., Stein, M.D., Savetsky, J.B., and Samet, J.H. (2000). "The doctor-patient relationship and HIV-infected patients' satisfaction with primary care physicians", *Journal of General Internal Medicine, 15*, 462-469.

Wanzer, M.B., Booth-Butterfield, M. and Gruber, K. (2004). "Perceptions of health care providers' communication: Relationships between patient-centered communication and satisfaction." *Health Care Communication, 16*(3), 363-384.

Zachariae, R., Pederson, C.G., Jensen, A.B., Ehrnrooth, E., Rossen, P.B., Von der Maase, H. (2003). "Association of perceived physician communication style with patient satisfaction, distress, cancer-related self-efficacy, and perceived control over the disease." *British Journal of Cancer, 88*, 658-665.

www.beckershospitalreview.com

http://journalofethics.ama-assn.org/2015/03/sectl -1503 .htm

16

Technology for Teaching

A Case Study on the Use of WhatsApp in Academic Activities of Higher Education System

P.V. Sangeetha *and* V. Anashwara

Introduction

The impact of technology has reflected in changing the different facets of life including education. Today, a teacher is considered as a facilitator. Surprisingly, teachers have realized this role and started using technology to improve their role of facilitating by making use of the new dimensions of technology. This study aims at how technology has facilitated the higher education system by analyzing the use of WhatsApp among the teachers and students.

WhatsApp is a mobile messaging application introduced by Brian Acton and Jan Koumin in the year 2009 with an aim of enabling simple, personal and real time messaging (Jisha and Jebakumar, 2014). WhatsApp helps its users to stay connected with their online contacts. Online exchange of images, PDF files, audio and videos is also possible through WhatsApp. What makes it different and superior among other medium is the connectivity and less cost. Ease of use and variety of options has made it a favourite to the society. Further, it made a rapid transformation in the way people communicate. People experience a new way of information-sharing activity which opened up many virtual discussion platforms. The research says that WhatsApp groups have the potential to be used as tutorial complements. According to Susilo (2014), WhatsApp has pedagogical, social and technological affordances, which allow putting up announcements, sharing ideas and resources, and implementing online discussions. As it offers immediate and instant dissemination of information, WhatsApp act as a potential platform for the learners to share curriculum related news and information.

Review of Literature

Method of teaching has changed a lot after the introduction of information and communication technology. Virtual classrooms are no longer a strange experience for the students. The role of teacher is transformed to facilitator. With the use of social media, teaching and learning is exploring its new dimensions. With the introduction and use of WhatsApp, 'Simple, personal and real time' has become the key word of campus too.

Instant messengers available in the application markets are capable of transmitting a wide range of messages with no restrictions on message lengths and also allow users to share multimedia like videos, location, images etc. All these services come at virtually no cost and one can avail this wide array of features for free simply by connecting the mobile device to the internet *via* data plans or WiFi connections. WhatsApp is the leader among the social networking by having 600 million users across the globe (Gudypaty and Jhala, 2015). Bouhnik and Deshen (2014) define WhatsApp as 'a smartphone application that operates on nearly all current types of devices and operating systems'. It was recently acquired by Facebook which has revised many features WhatsApp already provides. WhatsApp synchronizes with the phone book of the user and allows him to send such messages to any contacts that have the same application installed on their device. Bouhnik and Deshen (2014) say that the distinctive feature of WhatsApp is the option to create a group and to communicate within its boundaries. The creator of the group becomes its 'Group Admin', a position to manage adding and removing participants without the need for approval from the group members. All members in the group enjoy equal rights. The application enables the participants to receive an alert for each message sent or, alternatively, to mute the in-coming alerts for the duration of 8 hours, a week, or a whole year.

Mobile internet was not that popular among youth until the launch of WhatsApp application. As much as 90 per cent of youth subscribe for mobile internet as the application works through internet access. As a means of sending and receiving messages to and from individuals or groups, WhatsApp includes a variety of functions, such as text messages, attached images, audio files, video files, and links to web addresses (Bouhnik and Deshen, 2014). Mobile providers ensure faster connection in their internet services and offer attractive and affordable schemes. WhatsApp has brought a boom for the mobile internet concept. After the arrival of WhatsApp, many youngsters who were not a user of mobile internet has shifted to the usage of 2G and 3G, thereby bringing a huge profit for the mobile service providers through their internet usage. The attractive offers that they provide fascinate even more youngsters making them available 24/7 online. The speed that the internet packages offer retains the set of youngsters to be the regular users. After the entry of WhatsApp as a quick messenger, many of the youngsters started purchasing smart phones/ android phones, and this resulted in a huge sale for the smart phone industry. Many mobile companies started launching smart phones at affordable rates. This also enhanced the sale of smart phones.

Young people use WhatsApp to communicate with their family and friends. The various features available and the great speed in sending and receiving messages are added advantages of WhatsApp. Researches state that students remain online for 16 hours a day and spend an average of 5 hours per day on their smart phones interacting with others through social networking applications. Youth find WhatsApp as a platform to team up. Almost 70 per cent of the students own smart phones and have started utilizing the full potential of smart phones (Tata Consultancy Services, 2013). According to Bansal and Joshy (2014) immediate feedback to the problem; opportunity to learn on move; provide deeper clarity on issues through discussions; revision of previously learned topics; learning from others problems; and availability of learning material all the time are the major benefits enjoyed by the students.

Jisha and Jebakumar (2014) say that majority of the youngsters remain online 24/7 to access WhatsApp, thereby getting in touch with their friends without missing any single message. All the respondents agreed that they use their mobile phone full time to access

WhatsApp. 96 out of 100 respondents rated mobile as a necessity of their life in a scale of 1 to 5. Majority of youngsters use WhatsApp to chat with friends followed by relatives. Majority of the youngsters agreed that they converse with more than 15 people a day through WhatsApp. Majority of respondents rated 5 on a 5 point scale for the features of WhatsApp like instant messaging, group texting and updating profile image and status on a regular basis. The usage of unlimited audio files and video files were given 3 on 5 point scale. The youth consider it as a perfect tool for intimate social relationship, update their status, and exchange their photos and videos. Many of them use it as a stress relief tool also.

Use of WhatsApp for educational purposes started recently when the students identified the scope of the medium especially during the examination time. Quick group communication was a boon to them as it could overcome the limitation of physical mobility for group study. However, it took some time for the teachers to try this medium as an extension of their teaching activity. Tennyson (2010) says that the integration of the media artefact by the tutor or teacher in an e-learning system was the technological factor that improved online social interaction among group members in learning communities. According to Bouhnik and Deshen (2014), WhatsApp's groups were oriented to at least four goals: communicating with students, grooming a positive atmosphere and a sense of belonging in the class, creating a dialogue, using and sharing a learning platform. The usefulness and ease of use are the major factors influencing students' participation and adoption of online interaction (Litchfield *et al.*, 2007).

Educational mobile tools have a great potential to help students construct and share information and knowledge for learning through computers or mobile devices (Pence, 2007). Preston and colleagues (2010) found that nearly 70 per cent of students state that they learn just as well in online learning communities such as WhatsApp groups, Facebook communities, Twitter chats and Google+ communities, as they do in lectures that are held in the classroom in the presence of other students. Kadirire (2009) defines m-learning as "a form or an extension of e-Learning, which can take place anytime, anywhere with the help of a mobile communication device such as a mobile phone, iPod or any such small portable device". M-learning is any sort of learning that happens when the learner is not at a fixed, predetermined location, or learning opportunities offered by mobile technologies (O'Malley *et al.*, 2003). Individuals are found as more productive when consuming, interacting with, or creating information, mediating through a compact digital portable device that the individual carries on a regular basis, has reliable connectivity, and fits in a pocket or purse (Wexler *et al.*, 2008). Individuals who are engaged in a working group believe that their needs can be satisfied through working cooperatively and collaboratively as a community (Rovai, 2002).

Mercier and Higgins (2013) examined the adoption of online cooperative and collaborative learning strategies in online communities to support mathematics learning activities and found that a number of factors influencing students' participation in cooperative and collaborative communities. Students are motivated and positively oriented to participate in online communities to share knowledge related to courses. The social presence of students in online communities is a pertinent factor that influences student's participation in those communities (Cheung *et al.*, 2008).

However, there are some drawbacks too. Yeboah and Ewur (2014) found that the usage of WhatsApp has impacted negatively on the performance of students in Ghana. High use of WhatsApp lead the students to lack of concentration, lack of productive time and it also results in destroying their interest towards studying and other physical activities. This is where the transformation of WhatsApp as a tool for education finds its new dimensions. However, there has not been a concrete study with respect to its use for knowledge transfer between teachers and students in college level. This research tries to find out the usefulness of WhatsApp in the communicaticn between teachers and students at college levels. This will help to bridge the research gap that exists with regard to use of this particular application which is extensively used by students and various reasons leading to its popularity. The study will also try to throw light on the advantages as well as the disadvantages that springs from the use of this application in this respect. The objectives of this study are:

- To understand the use of WhatsApp for information exchange among students and teachers.
- To find the benefits of using WhatsApp for educational purposes.

- To identify the format in which maximum knowledge transfer occurs (images, videos or text).
- To understand the challenges/limitation of using WhatsApp for educational purpose.

Theoretical Perspective

According to Cross (1998), a community is a group of people who cooperate and collaborate each other in the activities. An online community also shares this feature in their teaching and learning activity. The major thrust of this community is to enhance the learning activity through constructive and collaborative way (Bielaczyc & Collins, 1999). People believe that the productivity and involvement are more when there are working as a group (Rovai, 2002). The present study has adopted activity theory to understand the usefulness of online teaching learning community. Activity theory is a framework which helps to analyse the kind of interaction among the online communities, their involvement and factors which affects their participation in the group discussion. Activity theory emphasises that learning through virtual discussion platforms features—involving a subject (the learners), an object (the task or activity) and tool or mediating artefacts and human behaviour is situated within a social context that influences their actions (Vygotsk, 1987).

Activity theory is based on six principles:

(1) The first principle is the orientedness of the object. The object here is the collaborative or cooperative learning in an online course.
(2) Subjects are actors engaged in activities. This is considered the individual level of activity theory; students are contextual subjects engaged in collaborative learning.
(3) Community or externalization is considered a social context of the system (e.g. a group of students engaged in learning based on social interaction for constructing and sharing of knowledge is an example of a learning community).
(4) Tools are considered a technological level of activity theory. In the system, communication between communities is mediated by tools that transmit social knowledge. It includes

the artefacts used by actors in the system. Tools influence actor-structure interactions and are influenced by culture.

(5) The division of labour is considered a hierarchical structure of activity or the division of activities among actors in the system.

(6) Rules are the conventions and guidelines regulating activities in the system, such as rules of discussion between students in collaborative learning (Barhoumi, 2015).

Researchers frequently use this framework to understand the human-computer interaction (Nardi, 1996). Many studies in the field of computer and mobile technology has used this framework to understand the structure, development and context of learning activities mediated by technologies and the determining factors of participation of the members in it (Hewitt, 2004), Strijbos and Fischer (2007), Lu and Churchill (2014)]. Activity theory is suitable for this research as it analyses the use of an online platform by teachers and students and also their involvement in the same.

Methodology

A Qualitative case study method has been used for the study. The main aim of this method was to explore the richness of experience of the respondents in using the WhatsApp for education purpose, the advantages they enjoy and the challenges they face in-depth and detail. For this purpose, in-depth interviews were conducted among the teachers in Madras Christian College, Chennai, India. The Madras Christian College also known as MCC, is arts and sciences college in Chennai, India. Founded in 1837, MCC is one of Asia's oldest extant colleges. Being the most liberal college among others in the city, MCC always has a vibrant teaching and learning community who are very active in adopting the latest technologies inside the campus. A sample of teachers was selected using snowball sampling method. All these teachers use WhatsApp groups through which they communicate with their students. Semi-structured interview schedule was used to understand the use, benefits and challenges teachers face in using WhatsApp for teaching learning purposes. The inclusion of open-ended questions helped the respondents to reveal their experience in the form of narration and it really helped the researchers to identify their vast experience and challenges of using WhatsApp in detail.

Three Focus group discussions were conducted among the students who are part of the WhatsApp groups in which the teachers interviewed are involved. Each group consisted of 8 to 10 participants. Students from multiple disciplines took part in the discussion. The students were selected using purposive sampling based on their active involvement in the group. The interviews lasted from 10 minutes to half an hour, while the focus group discussion lasted for 20 minutes. The samples were asked to respond to nine pre-prepared questions. However, in course of the conversation, additional questions were asked to keep the respondents on track and to obtain more clear answers from the interviewees.

Profile of the Sample

The respondents from the teaching community were 15 in number including 6 males and 9 females. The age group ranges from 29 to 56. All of them use WhatsApp for teaching learning purposes on a regular basis. Most of them act as the administrator of the group also. (Table 16.1)

Table 16.1: Profile of the Teachers

Profile of Teachers						
Name	*Gender*	*Age*	*Department*	*Admin*	*No. of groups*	*No. of members*
N1	Male	56 years	Zoology	Teacher	1	35
N2	Male	24 years	English	Teacher and student	1	32
N3	Female	29 years	Commerce	Teacher and student	2	45
N4	Female	26 years	Biology	Student	1	35
N5	Female	25 years	Zoology	Student	1	25
N6	Female	31 years	English	Teacher	2	30
N7	Female	30 years	Maths	Teacher	1	22
N8	Male	36 years	English	Student	1	30
N9	Male	24 years	Computer Sciences	Student	1	50
N10	Female	30 years	English	Teacher and student	3	21
N11	Male	33 years	English	Teacher	1	20
N12	Female	36 years	Social Work	Student	1	35
N13	Male	28 years	English	Teacher and student	1	20
N14	Female	29 years	Commerce	Teacher	1	45
N15	Female	35 Years	Media Studies	Teacher and student	2	33

The respondents for the focus group consist of the students who use WhatsApp for the educational purpose. Their age group is 18-22 including Degree and PG Degree students. There were 12 males and 14 females.

Findings

This research is done as an extension of an already conducted research, "WhatsApp Goes to School: Mobile Instant Messaging between Teachers and Students" by Bouhnik and Deshen (2014) of Bar-Ilan University, Ramat Gan, Israel. However, this is an attempt to find out the popularity and usefulness of the application in the higher education in India. Such a difference has its own importance in the very first sight in the sense that college students have more access to smartphones and WhatsApp than school students. Also, college students have higher level of maturity which determines the way in which they behave in virtual discussion platforms. As a result of these and many other factors, this research is bound to have results that are very much different from the results of the research by Bouhnik and Deshen.

All the teachers who were interviewed for the present study, uses WhatsApp to communicate with their students regarding educational purposes, but with varying degrees of involvement. In many, the students are the managers of the group. A few groups are managed by the teachers alone. Although these WhatsApp groups were formed only mainly to pass on information related to the curriculum, all the interviewees agreed that the use of WhatsApp brought out greater positive results than they thought. There number of participants in these WhatsApp groups varied and also, in some groups, students from different departments were present.

The major findings are,

- Teachers and students explore the technology of WhatsApp to its advantage to use it for teaching purposes. The teachers use WhatsApp to exchange immediate information to the students, mostly information like the time-tables, the curriculum, important announcements, the attendance status etc. and also to clarify doubts. Some teachers use the application to manage certain groups like the reading groups. However, one among the teachers goes a step further to use the application to conduct examination. The teachers attribute to the connectivity, low cost and easy accessibility of the application for it being employed in the teaching process. Teachers and students often indulge in long discussions over topics within the WhatsApp group. However, it is to be noted that the discussions are not confined to the group, but they are carried on to the classroom.

- The teachers stressed upon the time, energy and paper-saving factors of the application. The students need not wait to meet the teachers the next day to get their doubts clarified. It is also easy to communicate with students over WhatsApp. It is very handy and WhatsApp is a platform where everyone is present. Even students who are little introvert in the class find it easier to communicate with other students and teachers over WhatsApp. Such an interaction later leads to better relationship between teachers and students. In case of certain class groups where students from different departments are involved, there is always a tendency for the students of the same department to stick with themselves and to refrain from communicating with the students of other departments. In such scenarios, teachers encourage discussions between the students of different departments over a common WhatsApp group. If it was not for such a set-up, students would take up more time to develop a rapport among them.
- Texts, images, videos, voice notes and links are employed within the interaction between teachers and students. Some of the teachers prefer to text, while some of the teachers use voice texts instead of texting where they have to type out long messages. Voice-notes help the senders and receivers feel as if they are indulging in a real conversation. Videos and images related to the topics under discussion in the class are sent through WhatsApp. Students circulate among themselves the images of notes while teachers mostly send the images of the important announcements that they receive which are mostly in the form of hardcopy. The participants in WhatsApp groups also send links to websites or videos

which are of common importance. With the latest version of WhatsApp, it is also possible to send documents; however, it is not so widely used by the teachers or students.

- It was the teachers who mainly noted out the disadvantages of the employment of the smartphone application in teaching process. They pointed out that there is a lack of decorum within the WhatsApp group. At times one or two students indulge in long chats which could be done within a private thread. Although there is the option to mute the group in order to avoid the phone from beeping with every message, most of the teachers pointed out this as one of the major disadvantages. Also, there is the issue of spam. Some students forward messages which are of no use to anyone. The timing of the messages is also an issue, when the students keep on chatting over the group even late during night. Sometimes, students also fight over the group, a situation in which the teachers have to take up the role of peacemakers. The students mentioned that WhatsApp tends the students to bunk the classes more for the reason that even if they are not present in the class, they will come to know about the developments through the group. Also, they will get the notes through WhatsApp even if they are absent. Another issue with the employment of such a virtual medium in education is that there are still some students who cannot afford a smartphone in order to access WhatsApp. Hence special care has to be taken to ensure that every student is informed about the announcements made in the WhatsApp group.

Conclusion

Like any other social networking platforms, WhatsApp was also mainly used for the purpose of entertainment and socialisation to a great extent. People socialise over WhatsApp, get connected with their dear ones who are miles apart. The application was also used for the immediate exchange of important information. The users found great amusement in sharing pictures and videos over WhatsApp. The greater deal of privacy that comes with WhatsApp over Facebook and other similar platforms made the users feel comfortable sharing their private moments only with handpicked audience. We saw lots of videos and images and forward texts being shared through WhatsApp. A great deal of discussion takes place over WhatsApp groups. Groups were created among family members, friends, colleagues and so on. Some companies even used WhatsApp groups to educate their novice workers. At times, people meet over WhatsApp groups, the kind of groups which serve them mutual purposes. However, rarely it was being employed in the field of education. This may be, to some reason that not all students are able to have smartphones or that students or teachers or even parents were sceptical about the use of smartphones and applications for educational purposes. However, this research shows that something that is only used for entertainment or similar mundane activities could be used for better causes. Teachers found out that WhatsApp is where all their students are available and to which they pay attention to and hence it could be used to connect with the student circle in an easier manner. In this way, the application and its use have attained a better meaning.

References

Bielaczyc, K. and Collins, A. (1999). "Learning communities in classrooms: a reconceptualization of educational practice." In C.M. Reigeluth (Ed.). *Instructional design theories and models, 2*, 269–291. Mahwah, NJ: Lawrence Erlbaum Associates.

Bouhnik, D. and Deshen, M. (2014). "WhatsApp goes to school: Mobile instant messaging between teachers and students." *Journal of Information Technology Education: Research*, 13, 217-231. Retrieved from http://www.jite.org/documents/Vol13/JITEv13ResearchP217-231Bouhnik0601.pdf

Cheung, W.S., Hew, K.F., and Ng, S.L., (2008). "Towards an understanding of why students contribute in asynchronous online discussions." *Journal of Educational Computing Research, 38*(1), pp. 29–50.

Cross, K.P. (1998). *Why learning communities? Why now. About Campus, 3*(3), 4-11.

Gudipaty, L.P. and Jhala, K.Y. (2015). "WhatsApp Forensics: Decryption of Encrypted WhatsApp Databases on Non Rooted Android Devices", *Information Technology and Software Engineering*, Vol. 5(2), Accessed from: http://dx.doi.org/10.4172/2165-7866.1000147

Hewitt, J. (2004). "An exploration of community in a knowledge forum classroom: an activity system analysis." In S.A. Barab, R. Kling, and J.H. Gray (Eds.), *Designing for virtual communities in the service of learning*, pp. 210–238. Cambridge: Cambridge University Press.

Jisha, K, Jebakumar, (2014). "WhatsApp: A Trend Setter in Mobile Communication among Chennai Youth." *IOSR Journal of Humanities and Social Science (IOSR-JHSS)*, Volume 19, Issue 9, pp. 01-06.

Kadirire, J. (2009). *Mobile learning demystified: The evolution of mobile teaching and learning*. Retrieved from http://informingscience.net/buy/product_info.php? products_id=80.

Litchfield, A., Dyson, L., Lawrence, E. and Zmijewska, A. (2007). "Directions for m-learning research to enhance active learning." In *ICT: Providing choices for learners and learning*. Proceedings, Singapore. Accessed from http://www.ascilite.org.au/conferences/singapore07/procs/litchfield.pdfs

Lu, J. and Churchill, D. (2014). "Using social networking environments to support collaborative learning in a Chinese university class: Interaction pattern and influencing factors." *Australasian Journal of Educational Technology*, *30*(4), 472-486.

Mercier, E.M. and Higgins, S.E., (2013). "Collaborative learning with multi-touch technology: Developing adaptive expertise", Durham University School of Education, Leazes Road, Durham, UK, *Learning and Instruction*, 25(2013) pp. 13-23.

Nardi, B. (Ed.). (1996). *Context and consciousness: Activity theory and human computer interaction*. Cambridge, MA: MIT Press.

O'Malley, C., Vavoula, G., Glew, J.P., Taylor, J., and Sharples, M., (2005). "Guidelines for Learning/Teaching/Tutoring in a Mobile Environment", *Pedagogical Methodologies and Paradigms*, WP, Nottingham: University of Nottingham, pp. 82. Data accessed from http://hal.archives-ouvertes.fr/docs/00/69/62/44/PDF/OMalley-2005.pdf

Pence, H.E., (2007). "Preparing for the real Web generation." *Journal of Educational Technology Systems*, *35*(3), pp. 347-356.

Preston, G., Phillips, R., Gosper, M., McNeill, M., Woo, K., and Green, D., (2010). "Web-based Lecture technologies: Highlighting the changing nature of teaching and learning." *Australasian Journal of Educational Technology*, *26*(6), pp. 717-728.

Rovai, A.P., (2002). "Development of an instrument to measure classroom community." *Internet and Higher Education*, 5, pp. 197–211.

Strijbos, J.W. and Fischer, F. (2007). "Methodological challenges for collaborative learning research." *Learning and Instruction*, *17*(4), 389-393.

Suslio, A. (2014). "Exploring Facebook and WhatsApp As Supporting Social Network Applications For English Learning In Higher Education", *Teaching and Learning in the 21st century: Challenges for lecturers and teachers*. Accessed from http://repository.widyatama.ac.id/xmlui/bitstream/handle

Tennyson, R.D. (2010). Historical Reflection on Learning Theories and Instructional Design, *Contemporary Educational Technology*, *1*(1), pp. 1-16.

Vygotsky, L.S. (1978). *Mind in society: The development of higher psychological processes*. Cambridge, MA: Harvard University Press.

Wexler, S., Brown, J., Metcalf, D., Rogers, D. and Wagner, E., (2008). *The e-learning Guild Report Mobile Learning*. Data accessed from: http://www.elearningguild.com/research/archives/index.cfm?id=132&action=viewonly

Yeboah, J. and Ewur, D. (2014). "The Impact of WhatsApp Messenger Usage on Students Performance in Tertiary Institutions in Ghana", *Journal of Education and Practice*. Vol. 5 (6), pp. 157-164. Data accessed from http://www.iiste.org/ Journals/index.php/JEP/article/view/11241/11555

Index